YOUR AMAZING BRAND STORY

HOW TO HELP MORE PEOPLE AND MAKE MORE MONEY

TIM WOOD

First published by Busybird Publishing 2021

Copyright © 2021 Tim Wood

978-1-922691-21-7 (hardcover)
978-1-922691-22-4 (ebook)

This work is copyright. Apart from any use permitted under the *Copyright Act 1968*, no part of this publication may be reproduced, stored in a retrieval system or transmitted in any form or by any means, electronic, mechanical, photocopying, recording or otherwise, without the prior written permission of Tim Wood. Every effort has been made to use material, names and titles under fair use laws. Any breaches will be rectified in future editions of the book. Enquiries should be made with the author.

Cover design: Busybird Publishing

Layout and typesetting: Busybird Publishing

Busybird Publishing
2/118 Para Road
Montmorency, Victoria
Australia 3094
www.busybird.com.au

To those who love a good story and want to use the same emotional magic in their business and professional life, this is for you.

CONTENTS

A note from Tim	1
Introduction	7

CHAPTER ONE
Everyone wants to be better — 15

CHAPTER TWO
so give them what they want — 37

CHAPTER THREE
like only your brand can give it. — 73

CHAPTER FOUR
Give them stories they will share — 103

CHAPTER FIVE
and the experiences they seek to live it. — 131

Next steps	161
Story Log	163
Acknowledgements	167

A note from Tim

My brain works differently.

It's not unusual for someone to find my keys in the fridge or the cheese in the cupboard. Find My Phone would be the greatest thing ever invented, if only I could remember the password. Surprisingly (or perhaps not), within this chaos I yearn for structure and routine. They bring predictable calm. Calmness enables space for the thing I treasure most: emotional connection.

No heart, no story, no connection.

I find this true in personal life and work life – it's the connection that matters and stories that make it possible.

The problem I've observed over the years is that most brands struggle to make a real connection with their audience and therefore struggle to create the results they desire. Increasingly, brands fall for the trap of talking about themselves. But the reality is people don't care. We're all way too busy sorting out our own lives to give any time or headspace to random third-party things like brands.

But creating and sharing Your Amazing Brand Story can change that. It's all about interpretation.

I wrote this book for two reasons:

> **Reason #1**: Because I want to work with you to help you implement everything you read in this book.
>
> **Reason #2**: To give you results upfront so I'm more likely to achieve reason #1.

In other words, if I can help you create better results in advance, you're more likely to hire us. That's one of the keys to creating Your Amazing Brand Story – impact first. More on that later.

The part of my brain that loves structure has broken this book into five chapters; each chapter is based on a simple line. When the lines are strung together it explains the journey we'll go on to create Your Amazing Brand Story.

> **Everyone wants to be better**
>
> **so give them what they want**
>
> **like only your brand can give it.**
>
> **Give them stories they will share**
>
> **and the experiences they seek to live it.**

Here's a snapshot of each chapter.

CHAPTER ONE: Everyone wants to be better,

We'll start by walking in the shoes of your audience and discovering what your audience *really wants*, as opposed to what they *say* they want or what you *think* they want. This is the secret sauce the most successful brands tap into. Understanding your potential to impact your audience at a much higher level transforms how you are perceived, and therefore your value, before you even begin.

CHAPTER TWO: so give them what they want

Every amazing story is anchored in a truth. In this chapter you'll discover your brand truth – where the impact you make aligns with your audience's greatest need. Your brand truth is the kernel to creating Your Amazing Brand Story.

CHAPTER THREE: like only your brand can give it.

Next you'll learn how the most successful brands frame their truth the way their audience wants to experience it. You'll discover how to wrap your truth in emotion, so your brand story connects and moves people to action.

CHAPTER FOUR: Give them stories they will share,

Here we'll bring all the pieces together and turn your truth and emotion into Your Amazing Brand Story. You'll learn the art and science to becoming a better storyteller as you shift your story from expected to amazing.

CHAPTER FIVE: and the experiences they seek to live it.

Finally (and most satisfyingly), you'll learn how to bring your brand story to life by designing experiences into your business. You'll discover how to create experiences that make your brand story *the story* that people are talking about.

My goal is for you to create Your Amazing Brand Story as you read. There are six workbook exercises spread through this book. As you complete each exercise you will be building your brand story. The book is purposely short and designed to be read over a few sittings. Some people prefer to read or listen to the whole book first before returning to the workbook exercises – up to you.

However, a word of caution before we begin: like a favourite old pair of shoes, a brand story is only as good as the quality of the components that go into making it. You can skip ahead to Chapter Four and learn to tell better stories, but when you walk away the proverbial shoes you've made won't last.

Instead, I suggest you read the book sequentially and learn the building blocks to creating Your Amazing Brand Story. Then, like a skilled cobbler, you can ply your trade at will.

A bit of lingo before we begin

I've avoided marketing jargon wherever I can, but there are two terms to get your head around.

Audience – Interpret the term *audience* throughout this book as it applies to you or your organisation. Which groups do you want to influence? It could mean consumers, customers, clients, patients, employees, employers, members, the media or government.

Brand story – This is what people know you for; it's what your audience believes about your brand. Brand story can apply to an organisation or an individual. The brand story formula you'll learn inside applies to both personal and company stories. For simplicity I refer to 'brand story' as applying to your business, but as you read, interpret it as its most relevant for you.

Like it or not, you've already got a brand story – your audience already believes something about you. But is the story doing what you need it to do? Is it clear and impactful? Is your brand story driving growth?

Stories arouse emotional responses. Emotions engage parts of your brain that enable new connections and spark creative thoughts. Case studies bring logic and proof to emotive expression. For these reasons, throughout this book I've woven in all kinds of personal and professional tales and examples, from companies big and small, in the hope I can connect with you, challenge your perspective, influence your beliefs and inspire you to create your own Amazing Brand Story.

If after reading this book you decide you want help creating Your Amazing Brand Story, then please get in touch by going here:

YourAmazingBrandStory.com

Helping people and brands create, tell and monetise their Amazing Brand Story is what we do every day. We're here to help.

Now let's make a difference.

INTRODUCTION

It was 1991, three years after leaving school. Life took a welcome turn.

For the last three years I'd explored the life of an actor – performing for schoolchildren around Melbourne (Australia) by day and working in a theatre restaurant by night. I loved it and knew I'd found my thing. Then I was accepted into the Western Australian Academy of Performing Arts (WAAPA), which was quickly becoming one of the most renowned performing arts schools in the country. I was tingling with excitement. I packed my bags and moved to the other side of the country.

In the first semester, the class of '94 – which included fourteen other bright-eyed, eager students – found ourselves in a classroom with the Department Head John Milson. 'Milson', as he was known, was an imposing dramatic figure, appropriately always dressed from head-to-toe in black, as if he was perpetually grieving. Milson had pointed, tobacco-stained fingernails that he used like tongs to delicately fetch Fisherman's Friends from a well-worn bottomless packet. To say he was theatrically intimidating is a massive understatement.

Now Hearts (Milson loved calling people *Heart* in his theatrical, smoky voice), *we will take turns to sight-read passages of Shakespeare.*

I went numb. I had always been able to avoid these moments. Reading was my nemesis. Sight reading was my living hell. Extra tutorials through school never improved my struggle with reading. Instead, I developed tricks, like memorising chunks of text and etching elaborate acronyms into the side of pencils for exams. I had gotten through my entire school life hardly reading a book and never being found out. Now this. It felt like that recurring nightmare I have of walking onto stage completely naked – my cue was coming, and I had to go on … no choice.

I was only at the second line, and it was all over. The incoherent words coming out of my mouth sounded like a faulty machine gun. I couldn't read the text and interpret the meaning at the same time. The sense of disappointment and embarrassment in the room was palpable. I looked at Milson; his chin had fully disappeared into his ample neck as he physically winced at the slaughtered verse I had laid before him. Milson brought an abrupt and brutal end to the tragedy with his trademark expression of disdain … *oh dear.*

My budding acting career keeled over and died, much like Macbeth himself but without the fanfare. My nightmare had become a reality. This was the real world, and I came to the sobering realisation that I didn't cut it.

The next day, as I reluctantly entered the hallowed foyer of the academy, Milson summonsed me. It was all over. *Monsieur de bois, my office.*

When someone gives you a nickname it usually means they're warming to you, right? What I initially took as 'Mr Wood' in French was later pointed out to me by my far more perceptive peers as a reference to my acting style – *wooden*. Needless to say, the nickname stuck.

Monsieur de bois, you need some help.

No kidding.

But Milson had softened – less Fisherman's Friend, more Butter-Menthol. He spoke about me seeing a speech specialist. I hadn't the faintest idea what that involved or actually meant, but I knew he was throwing me a lifeline. I grabbed it.

That afternoon I sat opposite a man named Nigel Rideout, the resident speech specialist at the academy – and little did I know at the time, the creator of the WAAPA theatre department, globally respected theatre coach, and voice mentor to many famous actors. I had never met anyone like him. He was as English and as proper as the Queen. I immediately warmed to his quirky, theatrical formalities.

He ran me through a series of sight-reading exercises. I stammered and struggled. Then he asked me to sing words instead, new words I hadn't seen, but to the tune of 'Mary had a little lamb'.

No problem, I could sing them easily. *What was happening?*

Nigel stopped, removed his half-moon glasses from the tip of his nose and carefully tended a teapot he had brewing. He poured us each a cup in the finest of china, then with cup and saucer in hand, he adjusted his cravat, sat down in his well-worn armchair, crossed his legs, and told me he suspected I had some degree of dyslexia.

What the …?

I felt empty, lost, and reassured all at the same time. This 'burden' I had hidden had a name and this 'guru' didn't seem the slightest bit concerned.

With his fine china perched gently in his lap, Nigel began to tell me a story. His story. I was mesmerised.

He shared his childhood ambition of wanting to be an actor but having a lazy right eye and going off to St George's Hospital in London to do exercises. With help and hard work, he was able to overcome it. He then explained what he suspected was happening in my brain. He shared tales of past students who had challenges like mine. He'd learnt that with some experimentation and persistence, others had found a way through. He told me he believed he could help me too, but that my progress would depend on my effort; my preparedness to do the hard, disciplined work. *If you apply yourself, I believe you can train your brain to work around it.* There was a ray of light in Nigel's words.

Nigel had made an immediate impact. He understood that I was terrified and somehow made me feel normal and inspired. We connected. That afternoon was the beginning of a wonderful friendship.

For the next six months, I spent time every day reading to the tick-tock of a metronome. At first, it was super-slow, sixty beats per minute – *syll-a-ble-by-syll-a-ble*. Bit by bit we inched it higher. After two months I was reading fluently but without expression. It was working. Nigel slowly added more techniques and gradually I could feel my confidence rising. I was starting to believe again that this could happen. I would visit Nigel on Saturday mornings for extra classes and pots of English tea in fine china cups. Our classes evolved from reading to the craft of sight-reading, and then finally and most satisfyingly, to the art of connecting with an audience through the oldest of crafts – storytelling.

That was the moment when I first saw how the jigsaw of storytelling works. The pieces were jumbled in my head, but they were all there, and my brain was exploding with sparks of connection and creativity. That familiar sense of inner belief returned. I was soaring. I knew the longer I could be coached by Nigel, the more I could learn and the better I'd be.

Each week we pulled stories and speeches apart and analysed what each one was about – its message and its truth. What tools had the writer used to convey that truth? How effective was it? Nigel taught me how to construct a story to make an audience care, how to build tension and how to resolve it, and how to tell my own story.

I started to understand that the raw power of *truth* is the kernel of every great story, and that storytelling is simply a vehicle to give people an *experience* and therefore make an *impact*.

After graduating I did my darndest to make performing my career. I had fallen head over heels in love with my girlfriend Emma. But for much of those performing years Emma and I were ships in the night. She would arrive home after working all day, just as I was leaving to start my working day. Our relationship was going nowhere fast – something had to give. I looked around at my peers – some were fast becoming household names. Most, like me, were living from one week to the next. I love performing, but not enough to deprive me of starting a life and a family with the love of my life. So in 1999, after ten years in the world of theatre, I asked myself … *where's the opportunity?*

I found it via a sideways move. I took my love of storytelling and retrained as a copywriter. Through a friend I picked up a month's work experience at a big Sydney advertising agency, where I worked on the pitch for the launch of what became Virgin Airlines in Australia. That got me a job in another ad agency in Melbourne. Suddenly I was writing ads for big brands, and the ads were airing on primetime TV. I was in heaven – ideas would roll out of my head at a rate that gave everyone else (and often myself) a headache.

But my favourite part of copywriting was looking at the sales results each week. Initially the results were average. I got better. Eventually, the results were strong. Consistently strong. That was when the penny dropped – when I first saw the connection between stories and sales. Between theatre and marketing. Between experience and impact. I had found my second love.

The craft of storytelling is laced with tools that enable you to grab attention and engage your audience in a heartbeat.

Over the following fifteen years I was luckily enough to work with some very talented people and test this theory with some incredible brands – in particular McDonald's, Nike and Krispy Kreme. I was able to push the boundaries and see how far this belief in storytelling could go. I discovered it has no limits – time and again, creating stories and experiences delivered results.

Working across the worlds of theatre and brand marketing for over thirty years has proved to me that the essence of creating impact, and in turn growth, is the same for a writer, a director, an actor, a marketer or a business leader. The first step is to find your *truth*: the greatest impact you can make on your audience. The second step is to present that truth in the context of what your audience wants – *your story*. People buy on emotion, not logic. Then you amplify your story by creating *experiences*.

That's the code to unlock Your Amazing Brand Story:

 + + =

TRUTH + STORY + EXPERIENCES = IMPACT

This is the credo the most successful brands in the world use, and the formula you'll learn in this book. Your crystal-clear brand story, and the experiences that flow from it, creates the intangible affect you have on others. This is your competitive advantage – the thing you become known for.

As my sage friend and business partner Bruce McKaskill taught me, *money follows impact*. If you genuinely prioritise the impact you want to make, beyond commercial gain, growth will follow. Impact is your north star; money is a welcome by-product.

In the words of Walt Disney, *we don't make movies to make money – we make money to make more movies.*

Let's create Your Amazing Brand Story so you can make a bigger impact. What you do with the growth that follows is up to you.

CHAPTER ONE

Everyone wants to be better

so give them what they want

like only your brand can give it.

Give them stories they will share

and the experiences they seek to live it.

The amazing thing about change

Life has a way of sneaking up on you and kicking you in the arse when you least expect it.

A month after Emma and I were married, life was pretty much perfect. Both of us were working day jobs – Emma as a social worker and me as a copywriter in an ad agency. Then life went off the rails. Just after Christmas 2001, Emma contracted meningitis, a potentially fatal disease that swells the fluid and membranes surrounding the brain and spinal cord. The problem was that we didn't know she had it.

We'd just moved into our first home in Melbourne, a single-fronted weatherboard workers cottage. It was cute, but a hot Aussie summer had arrived, and our little home was now a fully functioning sauna. The ceiling desperately needed insulation.

I'm no DIY expert, and I'm also inherently frugal. I have learnt the hard way that these two facts are not a great combination, but there was no way I was going to pay someone $800 to waltz around our ceiling and lay insulation batts. How hard can it be?

What happened next was unfortunate on several levels.

In my wisdom, I decided to engage the help of my even more DIY-incompetent friend, Bloomy. With Bloomy providing moral support, I roped together a series of ladders to climb onto the pitched, corrugated iron roof and remove a sheet of metal so Bloomy could pass up the insulation batts for me to lay. What could possibly go wrong?

I was determined to get the job done before the heat of the afternoon sun. The makeshift ladder structure was like building scaffolding you might see in a developing nation. But despite itself, it seemed to do the job. Emma came to inspect the progress. Upon seeing me perched atop the precarious ladder configuration, she burst into tears and screamed, *they make TV commercials about this sort of thing*, then disappeared inside.

It's important to note at this point that I'm somewhat of a contrarian. If someone says *white*, I'll likely say *black*, just 'cause. Despite the timely observation from my newlywed, I pushed on. I was firmly set on having a more comfortable home that day. It was much later I came to appreciate the term 'happy wife, happy life'.

So with two sheets of metal off and insulation batts in hand, I took my first tentative steps into the roof. Five paces in, my foot slipped off the beam I was teetering on, and I fell straight through the plaster ceiling – no broken bones, just a shattered ego.

At this point, both Bloomy and Emma were in tears. Bloomy had never seen something so funny, but Em was now beyond despair. She went to bed that afternoon and slept for four days. I thought she was dirty with me, and I didn't pick up on the signs – massive headache, sensitivity to light and noise, and not eating or drinking. What I didn't realise was she was in a semi-coma. Even now, I feel sick thinking about it. On day five, I took her to the doctor; she was diagnosed with meningitis and spent the next four months at home recovering.

By the way, the ceiling cost twice as much to repair as it did to have a chap come and install the insulation batts (that hurt).

Changing location

Em's brush with fate was one of those life-changing moments that brings perspective – and with it, gratitude and clarity. It made us both think about what mattered. We both wanted a life full of experiences together. We realised we each had the same dream – to live in another country and experience other cultures. So, we quit our jobs and we headed for London.

On 24 July 2002, two eager thirty-ish-year-olds arrived in London, ready to find jobs – Emma as a social worker or family therapist, and me as a marketer. It hadn't occurred to us that the UK closes down over their summer break. No jobs going – so we backpacked around Europe for a month (awesome fun!). At the start of September, we started looking for work again. Emma picked up a job quickly – Aussie trained social workers were in high demand, and she was well qualified. It was good money, but not enough to cover two people living in London.

While Emma was heading up, I was heading down. I just couldn't get a job. I pulled every string I could muster. By December that year, I was still jobless. Apparently, if you haven't worked in London before, you haven't worked. As the cost of surviving in

London took its weekly toll, the decision to sign a twelve-month lease on our little apartment was weighing heavily on both of us. Our bank account was eroding before our eyes, and along with it, my sense of confidence. For twelve weeks I had worked the beat and had nothing to show it. We had one month of savings left before eating into our airfares home.

In late November, as our first cold London winter was setting in, a friend of a friend invited us to go out with a group of his friends. We couldn't afford it, but at the same time we couldn't afford *not* to go. So, we went.

At the pub I sat next to an older guy, maybe in his mid-sixties. His name was Jerry, a long-time ad-man at one of London's top advertising agencies. I told him about my journey of desperately trying to find a job. He sat and listened to me bleed my heart out. Then he gave me two pieces of advice that changed everything.

The first thing he said was, *stop being so miserable*. When an Englishman tells you you're miserable, you know you're in trouble. He said, *get a job, any job. It's easier to find work when you're in work, and you'll stop being such a misery-guts*.

Thanks Jerry, point taken.

The second piece of advice he gave me was more profound. *You're going about job-hunting the wrong way. You're trying to be like everyone else so you're blending in. Instead, understand who you are to stand out. Change your thinking and you'll change your results.*

He said he'd learnt over the years that nearly everything people engage with is in the pursuit of the change they seek. We all want to evolve, be better, sometimes even transform. And so intuitively, we all seek out people and brands that can help us achieve this. The brands that win are those which can best deliver the change people seek.

It's different for each person but the essence is the same. We each want to change. To grow. To thrive. It's true for anything with which we engage: a pair of shoes, beauty products, a course, a meditation retreat, a new car, a soul mate.

Jerry painted the picture of a job interview or a pitch scenario – instead of thinking about the change *I* sought, step into the other person's shoes. What's the change *they* seek? What's the feeling *they* want to experience? We buy the solution that will help us evolve, be greater or even help us transform – and usually we don't even know it. These things are not functional; they're intangible. So, instead of playing the '*I'm just like everyone else but better*' card, and blending into the pack, the secret is to understand the most powerful effect you make on others and how to position yourself to deliver that. *Tell your story through their lens. Accentuate your differences. Think bigger and enable yourself to be the change, the transformation, the inspiration that they're seeking.*

I was speechless.

I'd never thought about what Jerry said from that perspective. In trying to solve my problem, getting a job, I was ignoring the fact that people buy the solutions to *their own* challenges. I was viewing the scenario through my eyes, not walking in the shoes of my audience. To fit in, I was squashing the essence of who I am instead of celebrating my differences and uniqueness to stand out. I was presenting myself as functionally competent, as opposed to engaging potential employers with the distinctive effect I can make on others and presenting it in the context of what they want.

My head was spinning.

Changing thinking

The next day I woke up to a dark and frosty London winter's morning. I felt renewed, telling Em that today I would get a job, any job. I figured my best chance of success was in retail. I'd worked in retail through university. I'm a people person and I know how to sell stuff – just not myself!

I took the tube to Hammersmith and came out on Kensington High Street. It looked as good a chance as any. I turned right, back towards Hyde Park because it gave me a few miles of Kensington High Street shops. I presented myself at every one that looked vaguely like me – department stores, sports stores, coffee shops, pubs, restaurants. By lunch I'd enquired at about thirty shops. Nothing. By 4 pm I'd given out fifty CVs, and a cold London evening was closing in yet again.

Next to the Kensington High Street tube station, I spotted a little store called Trotters. Its bright piggy logo stood out like a beacon in the dreary dusk of London; they sold children's clothes, cut children's hair and fitted children's shoes. I love kids, can't cut hair and have zero fashion sense. Shoes it was.

I found the shoe section at the back of the long skinny store. There was a stern, matriarchal looking woman, re-arranging the shoe shelf in an otherwise empty section of store. *People want change. They want you to bring the change they desire.* I introduced myself. She was steelier than she looked. Ice-lady. She asked me if I'd ever fitted children's shoes. I told her, *I'm a shoeologist.*

The rarest hint of a smile appeared on her face. *And what exactly does a 'shoeologist' do?*

A shoeologist, I said, *sells lots and lots of shoes.*

She chuckled. *Be here tomorrow at 9 am, and we'll see how you go.*

The pay was ordinary, but I had a job. Jerry was right; the spring was back in my step.

Changing results

But it's what Jerry said about *knowing who you are, and enabling others to be better*, that intrigued me most. *People buy the solution to the change they seek.* Is that true? Over the years that followed, I explored this theory. I came to the conclusion that all people do, in fact, seek change. But more than that, I arrived at the belief that the desire to be better is the single biggest driving force behind every decision we make as human beings. And usually, we're not even conscious of it.

The choices we make reflect the change we seek – be that self-perception or the perception of others.

We seek to be wiser, calmer, more patient or more present. We strive to be more grounded, more beautiful, more prestigious, smarter or handier; whatever it is, we all seek change. We seek the sated feeling it evokes inside us. Therefore, we hunt and hold dear to us the people or brands that can deliver this change.

In seeking a marketing job in London, I focused on my needs – the change I desired. I was transactional – here's my CV, *here's who I am, where I studied, whom I've worked for and what I've done.* That was my core challenge, the change I wanted. This was a far cry from the change any potential employer sought.

So, I tweaked my story to be true to who I was and position myself as the answer to their problem. I still had all the functional stuff on my CV, but across the top, in big bold letters, I put a headline – *I'm a storyteller who brings brand experiences to life.* That's the story I started telling. I knew I'd narrow the field, but

I also now knew that I'd stand out, and could deliver on my headline in spades.

On my lunch breaks from fitting the umpteenth pair of Mary Janes, I would make calls, meet recruiters and send out CVs. We kept our heads above water through our first London winter. In late February, I got lucky. My good friend Michael Scott suggested I apply for a job at the UK headquarters of McDonald's. They needed a marketer who understood children and performance. I got the gig. I was working in the Happy Meal team with the task of making Ronald McDonald cool again. My honest gut reaction was that it might be easier to bring Shakespeare back from the dead. No matter, I was back in the game.

The desire for change, to evolve and feel different, runs through our lives every day in the decisions we make. Often unconsciously. Understanding this need in your audience and positioning your brand to deliver what they want is the keystone for business growth. I've learnt that uncovering what your audience really wants is about asking the right questions.

Nobody cares about your brand

Most marketers start by asking, *how can I make my brand better?* While that's the goal, it's not the right question to ask. The marketing world is obsessed with the concept of brands. However, the reality is that life is way too noisy, complex and busy, and people far too egocentric, for customers to give much head space to brands.

But …

When you frame what you do in the context of what your audience *wants*, you change the game. And in the process, you transform your value.

This is the important distinction most people miss: when brands talk about themselves first, including what they do and how they do it, audiences switch off because, quite frankly, it's boring. The storyteller is not interpreting how the story is relevant in their customer's life.

However, when brands present the impact they make within the context of the change their audience seeks, it immediately resonates. People don't buy a product or service in isolation. They buy the change they believe it can make in their lives.

Consider this:

- Colgate doesn't sell toothpaste. Colgate gives you confidence.

- IKEA doesn't sell flat-packed furniture. IKEA makes your home look better.

- Red Bull doesn't sell energy drinks. Red Bull gives you wings.

When a brand's story revolves around a commodity, the brand misses the opportunity to transform their perceived value. Sustained growth will arrive when you create an emotional story that accompanies the rational reasoning for the decision to buy.

The truth about McDonald's

McDonald's knows something about parents of young children that the parents are probably not even conscious of themselves.

Parents aren't buying a Happy Meal solely because it's a meal in a box. While that's a good, functional reason, it's not the real reason. McDonald's discovered the intangible reason some time ago and has been delivering it in spades ever since.

When I first joined McDonald's, I was sent to work in stores for two weeks, exposing me to every facet of store operations. That was followed by another two weeks of understanding the machinations behind the shop front that keeps stores humming. Understanding what the consumer wants at the coalface is embedded in the McDonald's ethos. Towards the end of my fourth week, I replaced the hairnet with a necktie and sat down with Sue, a mother and McDonald's Happy Meal doyen.

So Tim, she said, *have you worked out why people buy Happy Meals?*

Well, you can feed a child for under three quid, I wisely offered. But Sue had seen the likes of me before.

That helps, but no, that's not the real reason. When parents choose a Happy Meal they are buying a moment to be a happy family together. End of story.

You know those occasions when a little bit of vomit comes up into your mouth? I nearly had it right there and then. Sue's been drinking the Golden Arches Kool-Aid, surely. Come on …

But I didn't fancy going back to fitting kids' shoes, so I zipped my lip and listened.

Sue explained that for parents of young children, *life's full of stress, angst and tension. Every day is a rollercoaster of emotions. It's bloody hard, tiring, thankless work. So, the idea that for fifteen minutes you can sit down and just be with your child – content, happy even, without the fighting and the screaming – is rather appealing.*

There it was again. An ethereal need that floated above the obvious functional requirement. By walking in the shoes of the McDonald's consumer, Sue had painted the picture of what a McDonald's family really wanted.

Stop and reward yourself – enjoy the moment.

This is the brand truth at the heart of the largest, most successful food franchise globally. The experiences McDonald's creates play out differently for its different audience segments, but the essence is the same.

Rewarding the young family market is core to the McDonald's business, which does a fantastic job of bringing this truth to life with lived experiences. McDonald's suburban stores have bright, colourful play equipment bursting out of them like beacons of joy and respite for young families driving past. Inside, the seating has 50s-style booths bringing children physically closer to their parents, providing comfort and security to children.

This is all done very consciously, based on the truth of reward and connection. The essence of the McDonald's brand is used as the filter for every consumer-facing decision they make. How it delivers its products and services become the stories people tell. It's rare to speak to someone who can't recall a special childhood memory of a family trip to McDonald's.

Humans buy on emotions and rationalise the decision with logic. The emotions are fuelled by the change they believe the purchase will make in their lives. The logic feeds the brain's need for rational sequence and order.

- Why do you drive the car you drive? What's the feeling it delivers for you? How does it impact how people perceive you or how you feel about yourself?

- Why do people get obsessed with job titles? It doesn't change what they do, but it does change how they are perceived and their perception of self. Job titles are an emotive status tag for what someone does; therefore, they are important.

When humans buy something, we seek way more than the commodity we purchase. We seek the change in feeling it gives us, or the change in perception of others. So people don't care about brands, until the brand gives them what they want – the change they seek.

When you walk in the shoes of your audience and understand the unconscious bias we all have to be better, to change, you can view your potential impact with the gravitas it deserves. Identifying this impact transforms your value – you move from selling a commodity to offering the emotional leverage your audience seeks.

Before we move on, it's important you throw your metaphorical 'brand rope' over the highest possible branch in the jungle. You'll achieve this in the first workbook exercise. Elevating your thinking before you begin means greater emotional leverage later – like Tarzan and Jane, throwing the rope high now means you'll swing much further when you take the leap.

Workbook Exercise 1:

Discover what your audience really wants

Do the following exercise by first writing down the answer to this question:

> *How do our products or services give our audience the change they seek?*

Write down the obvious answer, which is usually the first thing that comes to mind. Now ask the follow-up question:

> *'How does [your answer] give our audience the change they seek?'*

Write down your answer. Continue to ask the follow-up question to each subsequent answer. This technique will force you to 'ladder-up' and elevate your perspective.

We did this exercise recently with a client who was preparing for a competitive pitch. The client's brand was in the entertainment sector. The exercise went like this:

> Starter question: How do your products or services give your audience the change they seek?
>
> First answer: They will sell more tickets.
>
> Ladder-up: How does 'selling more tickets' give your audience the change they seek?
>
> Second answer: It makes them more profitable.
>
> Ladder-up again: How does 'greater profitability' give your audience the change they seek?
>
> Third answer: It will provide them much needed kudos as a successful commercial entertainment company.
>
> Ladder-up again: How does 'greater kudos' give your audience the change they seek?
>
> Fourth answer: It will bring them far greater influence in the sector.

Keep going until you run out of elevation, then look at your answers and circle the greatest change your audience desires that you can genuinely lay claim to.

In the example above our client decided the biggest desired change they could impact was *greater kudos*. They knew their client desperately wanted the kudos that would accompany successful ticket sales. In their pitch our client wove the emotional narrative of *greater kudos* throughout their presentation. The pitch was already functionally excellent; the thread of *greater kudos* shifted the tone from expected to inspirational.

They elevated their offer and won the pitch.

In the next chapter we'll add more business rigor to finding your truth, but for now I want you to be open to the possibility that your audience's strongest need is emotion, status or credibility driven. Despite the logical, rational reasoning you currently hear from them, it's the person or brand that evokes the most powerful emotional connection that gets the sale.

When you create emotional leverage, you transform your value. To anchor your brand's emotional leverage points in fact, we must begin with truth and that's what we'll do next.

Key chapter takeaways

- When you frame what you do in the context of what your audience wants, you transform your value.

- When you reveal the greatest emotional change your audience seeks (that is, how they want to be better), you unlock the potential value of your brand.

- To achieve this, you must separate the functional and logical needs of your audience from their emotional or intangible needs.

- People buy the change they believe your brand can make in their lives.

CHAPTER TWO

Everyone wants to be better

so give them what they want

like only your brand can give it.

Give them stories they will share

and the experiences they seek to live it.

Begin with truth

Give 'em what they want. I love this expression. I suspect its origins date back to early show biz times when savvy impresarios blended creativity with business. You can almost hear PT Barnum or Cameron Mackintosh commanding this of their people. Both these men had an uncanny ability to package creativity into heart-stopping entertainment. But the truth to their success lived in first knowing the incredible effect they could make on others. Then, they'd package it to inspire and enthral audiences, resulting in a cash-cow for producers.

This is what we call your *truth* – the intersection of the greatest impact you can have on your audience and the greatest impact they seek. When you find this apex, the sparks begin to fly – or, in business terms, demand exceeds supply.

Your story is a vehicle used to bring the truth to life with emotion – much like a song, play or movie are emotional vehicles to deliver a truth.

Remember the formula to unlock growth:

Truth + Story + Experiences = Impact

Understanding the truth behind another brand can make the process of revealing your own brand truth easier. For me, this happens when I stumble across a brand story that is so blaringly concise and integrated into a business, it makes my heart sing.

The little door of magic

Wandering the streets of Madrid, I saw a little girl leap out of their stroller and run, with teddy in hand, to a retail shop. The child had obviously spotted someone special in her life and was making a dash for a big cuddle.

But no.

She ran straight into a store, through a special child-sized door that was next to a normal door. The little girl had no sooner disappeared than she reappeared and did it all again. Her mother caught up and they entered the store together, through their respective doors – adult and child watching each other, connected through loving grins.

I couldn't believe what I'd just seen. The magnetism of this little door had created a moment for this child and her mother. I discovered that on the other side of the child's door was a little tunnel that landed the girl in the middle of toy heaven. The store is called Imaginarium, where children playing with toys on the shelves is encouraged.

Imaginarium specialises in education and play for children. Since its origins, Imaginarium believes that *play is an essential part of children's development, health, learning, and happiness*. That's its truth. The stores express this through their brand story: *We make a better childhood easier for everyone.* That's exactly what I just saw in the experience the little door created.

Using its truth as its inspiration, Imaginarium has created an experience that *makes a better childhood easier for everyone*. They didn't talk about it, they did it. Bingo, job done. No need for clever marketing words behind the shop counter.

The story is baked into the shop front. The little door creates an experience for children and parents that lives on in their hearts.

That's our aim: to find your truth, then bring it to life through the simplicity of stories and experiences so your audience knows exactly what it is you want to be known for – in a heartbeat.

Truthful questions

To uncover your brand's truth, the two questions to ask are:

1. What's the greatest impact our brand can make on our audience?

2. What's the greatest impact our audience seeks?

An audience is only valuable if they have a *want* you can solve – an itch you can scratch. The bigger the want, the greater the impact. When the impact you can make and the impact your audience seeks are aligned, you reveal your brand truth.

The diagram on the following page plots this on a X–Y axis. Many brands occupy the top-left quadrant where the impact is high, but the audience demand is medium or low. When we hear clients say, *the people who buy from us love us … but not enough people buy*, it's usually because they are entrenched in this quadrant.

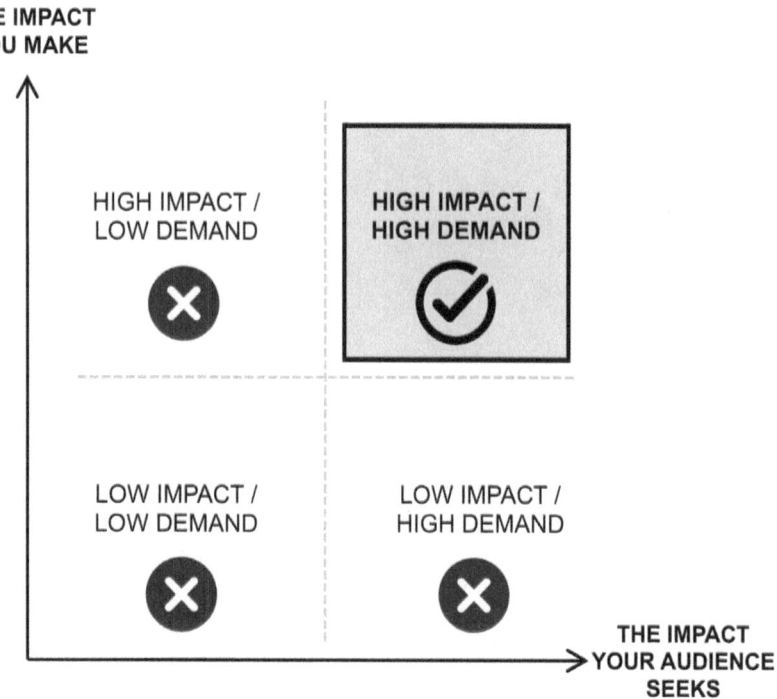

Conversely, when a brand is price and/or volume dependant it usually indicates their business resides in the bottom right quadrant – lower impact / higher demand. Such businesses work hard for every dollar and are continually at risk of a competitor under-cutting them. The lack of emotional impact on their audience serves as a glass ceiling to their commercial success – often they have commoditised their brand.

Aligning your greatest impact with the greatest impact your audience seeks is exactly the process our agency used to help transition an established brand that had lost its meaning into a life-saving powerhouse.

Soccer, silence and sirens

When a father had a heart attack on the side of a soccer pitch in Melbourne in 2016, he had no idea that the decision St John Ambulance Victoria (SJAV) had taken seven years earlier would save his life.

It was a winter weekend like any other for Melbourne soccer families, with parents congregating for ritualistic small talk, bad coffee, and banal comments on the weather.

In the distance, I saw a man collapse, then everything immediately went into slow motion for me.

Seven years earlier, SJAV had wanted corporate sponsorship, but they couldn't get it. They tasked our agency to help them. It was obvious to our team that there was a far bigger problem – and a far greater opportunity that SJAV wasn't seeing. What followed in the five minutes after the man's collapse can be traced back to the actions SJAV took all those years earlier.

A woman stepped in and started CPR on the man. She was strong and confident, issuing instructions to those around her as she methodically and vigorously pumped the man's chest.

Someone retrieved a defib machine from the clubrooms and laid it next to the man.

When the ambulance arrived, the paramedics saw the best sight they could hope for: a middle-aged man sitting up and chatting, with a used defib machine sprawled out next to him.

What our team had discovered all those years ago was that despite SJAV's commercial success, there were fundamental inhibitions to growth. Clarity of the problem is the first step to creating an impactful solution. What SJAV faced was complex, not least of all the disconnect between those who benefited and those who paid.

However, when you boiled it all down, our team identified that four key factors were causing the challenges.

1. SJAV's pursuit of revenue was over-riding their desired impact – there was no *truth* guiding their actions.

2. SJAV had no clearly identified *audience*; in fact, they served everyone and anyone.

3. No one knew what SJAV stood for other than a fee for service – SJAV desperately lacked a clearly defined *brand story*.

4. And because of all this, they were not creating *experiences* that impacted their audience in ways that spread the word.

Essentially, they were a cause without a cause.

But the pathway out was clear. Growth would come from applying the formula:

Truth + Story + Experiences = Impact

SJAV did what too few do; they turned insight into action in the form of a bold, ambitious story.

To define their truth, SJAV went back to their roots – to revisit the biggest impact they could make. It was obvious: *to deliver first-aid that saves lives*. Then they worked out who SJAV could have the greatest impact on – in other words, who needed this most. SJAV decided young families wanted safety and the knowledge of what to do when things go wrong and would become their primary audience.

SJAV arrived on the powerful story of *first-aid that saves lives*. Over the next five years, SJAV created *experiences* that brought this story to life. They invested over $3 million in free or subsidised defibrillators across Victoria and started providing first-aid training to 200,000 primary school students each year, for free.

The woman who took control on that day was first-aid trained. The defib machine had been gifted to the club by SJAV a year earlier. The man was released from hospital a week later.

The unsung heroes of this story are the board and senior executive team at SJAV back in 2009. They had the courage to stare down the truth and embrace the opportunity. The consequences of their actions have saved an incalculable number of lives, and profoundly brought meaning to a struggling brand. They no longer want nor need corporate sponsorship.

Oh, and I nearly forgot the punchline. Since making the changes, SJAV's revenue almost doubled in the first ten years.

Money follows impact.

Create your master key

The greatest impact you can make is the essence of who you are – the key, if you like. It's often the thing that ignites the fire in your belly and makes you remarkable; it's the reason you get out of bed every morning. It's your ambition beyond commercial gain. If you lose sight of this, as I did while job-hunting in London and as St John Ambulance Victoria did, you risk becoming homogenous and drifting back into the pack – the very antithesis of having a point of difference. This is not an exercise in compromising – it's an exercise in generating growth.

When you take the time to define your greatest impact, then frame it with the knowledge of what an audience wants and values, you create your competitive advantage. Now you have the master key to unlock greater impact.

When a brand story delivers the change an audience seeks, the brand stands out and stories spread. Your brand story becomes amazing – that's the goal.

Reflect on what you discovered in the previous chapter – the biggest change your audience seeks is where the opportunity to connect exists. This is a process of peeling back the layers of the truth onion and testing it against what you know to be true about your audience and your brand. In a moment you're going to discover your brand truth, but first there's a very important question to answer.

Who's your target audience?

Red Nose

Being very specific about your primary audience before you ask what they want is critical. This clarity of who you're targeting (and why) is often overlooked. It was this step that led to a lightbulb moment for one of Australia's most successful community organisations and triggered significant change. Here's their story.

Suburban Melbourne, 1977.

You're living in *The Golden Years*. You and your partner have four young children, the eldest is five and half years old, the youngest only eight months. They're all full of life and mischief, just as kids should be.

Like any parent, you're making it up as you go and doing your darndest to make every post a winner – parenting, working, surviving. It might not always feel like it, but life's good. Then one day you find your youngest child dead in their cot.

This is the tragic and inspiring story of the Fitzgerald family: parents Kaarene and Kevin and their children Karl, Anita, Lacey and Glenn.

I met Kevin forty years after Glenn's death from SIDS (sudden infant death syndrome). Our agency had been tasked to help the foundation that Kaarene and Kevin founded, which later became known as SIDS and Kids.

I'll let Kevin tell his story.

> When we found Glenn in his cot, we tried everything. I did mouth to mouth, trying to get anything to happen, but there was nothing there. It's just the most terrible feeling when you have a baby who last night you cuddled and today he's just a rag doll. It's just awful.
>
> At the Royal Children's Hospital, we just wanted to know why this happened. And it was something that no one could tell us why. So, we started saying we have to do something about it. We have to know. If this happens to other people, then it's just terrible because there's no support, nothing.
>
> The doctor at the Children's Hospital suggested we do something like start a foundation. We knew we had to raise money to fund research and get support for people. So on that day, the day after Glenn died, we started the foundation.
>
> I remember doing a radio interview, and the presenter asked, what can people do? Who can

they call? At the time, the only phone number available was our home number. So I said, you can talk to Kaarene and me. And the phone just started to ring. It would ring from 8 am to 8 pm. We'd stop for a quick dinner, and then keep going.

Through research, SIDS and Kids identified the six safe sleeping guidelines which led to Back to Sleep, the national public health campaign that has helped reduce SIDS in Australia by 85% since 1989. Kevin credits Kaarene's natural leadership for the success – *she was a dominant force*. To this day, the research is still referenced globally as best practice. This research, combined with the tireless efforts of others – many of them bereaved parents themselves – in educating and advocating for new parents, is responsible for an incalculable number of lives saved around the world.

When our agency entered the frame, we saw that the sign out the front no longer matched what was happening inside SIDS and Kids. The incredible knowledge and skills developed to reduce SIDS had morphed and amplified and was now being applied way beyond sudden infant death syndrome alone, to research and help prevent *all sudden and unexpected deaths in infants and children*. By sheer weight of numbers, this was a problem manifestly larger than SIDS in isolation. But the organisation was still known as the 'SIDS people'.

The challenge? SIDS and Kids was no longer *saying what they do or doing what they say*. Their brand story needed to be realigned to communicate a clear message once again, sending clear signals to the people who mattered and raising the funds required to save more lives.

After an immersive process with the team, Red Nose was created as the new organisational brand going forward. Their truth: *A future where no child dies suddenly or unexpectedly.* Their new brand story was simple: *saving little lives.*

In 2019, Red Nose was awarded significant funding from the federal government when it was announced as the lead organisation to launch a national health promotion focusing on building awareness of stillbirths – and the appropriate risk prevention strategies for new and expecting parents. In late 2020, Red Nose merged with SANDS, an organisation on a similar path; this added knowledge, expertise and resources to help save more little lives.

The important work continues.

A story without an audience is not a story – it's like singing in the shower. Defining the right target audience can be the difference between success and failure.

This next exercise will give you a strong indication if you're focusing on the right target audience for Your Amazing Brand Story.

Workbook Exercise 2:

Define your target audience

Who's your current target audience? Picture them clearly in your mind.

Now answer 'yes' or 'no' to these four questions. I urge you to be ruthless in your answers; sugar-coating reality now will increase your chances of diabetes later.

1. Do you spend 80% or more of your resources targeting only this audience? Yes / No
2. Are they the most valuable audience for you to target? Yes / No
3. Will impacting this audience alone deliver the growth you require? Yes / No

4. Is your consumer (the end-user of your product or service) the same as your customer (your primary source of revenue)? Yes / No

How many 'yes' answers did you tally? Analyse the strength of your target audience using this table:

'Yes' Answers	Suggested action:
4	You're ready to define your brand truth.
3	Focusing on your 'no' answer, consider what would need to happen to change it to 'yes'. If you answered 'no' to question 4, be aware of the different needs of the customer and consumer as you create your brand story. Priority of focus should be given to the consumer (the end user). Having influence and 'ownership' of the end user increases your influence with the customer (the payer).
0–2	I'd suggest there are fault lines in your current target audience or resource allocation that are inhibiting growth. Reconsider both and run the exercise again until the 'yes' responses dominate.

Once your target audience is clearly defined, give them a persona – we call this your audience Avatar. Get to know your Avatar intimately and give them a name – say it's *Sam*. What's Sam's gender, age, income, education, family status, likes, dislikes, attitudes, and behaviours? Is there a through line to your target audience that defines *Sam*: what's their ambition, their greatest pain point, or need, or fear?

To make this task (and others that will follow) easier, we've created a toolkit of additional resources you'll find in the link below. For this exercise, use the audience Avatar template that has a mock Avatar example included. Take the time to fill it out. Later you'll use this information to create Your Amazing Brand Story. You can access the template here:

YourAmazingBrandStory.com/toolkit

With your audience Avatar fleshed out, now it's time to define your brand truth.

To find your truth it's important to adopt an elevated perspective. Remember that brand rope you threw over the highest branch earlier? You're about to swing. A lofty mindset going into this next exercise will help, so let me try and lighten the mood a little by sharing one of my favourite stories about finding one's brand truth.

Connections

Back in my uni days, one of the requirements of each student graduating from WAAPA was to raise $1,500 to fund a showcase tour on the east coast of Australia. The money would cover airfares, hotels and transfers. With stars in their eyes, the graduating class each year would perform for agents and producers in the desperate hope of kick-starting their professional career.

For the previous two years, I had watched final year students do cake stalls week after week to raise their funds. This immediately struck me as odd ... these wonderfully trained, incredibly gifted actors, singers and dancers all doing their best Martha Stewart impersonations, trying to flog cakes to students who had no cash.

With the benefit of hindsight, I can now tell you that they had identified neither the biggest impact they could make, nor an audience that wanted that impact. The result was a disjointed story that suffered terribly.

Hello fellow uni student, I'm an actor trying to raise money so I can be discovered. Do you want to buy a cake?

At the beginning of our final year at WAAPA, I posed a thought to my peers: how could we use the skills and talents we have, to make raising the cash we need both easier and a lot more fun? All up, we needed $18,000. None of us had ever had this much money in our lives, let alone knew how to make that in profit.

We brainstormed all kind of ideas, like putting on a show and selling tickets to the public, or creating private performances in the homes of wealthy, art-loving Perth folk. But as we pondered each idea, reality would bite; who would buy enough tickets to make $18,000 when even the local theatre company is struggling to draw big crowds? What made us think we could attract a big enough or wealthy enough audience to make this happen?

The cake stall was unfortunately looking like the best option.

One day after a dance class, a few of us stayed back and sat in the studio. How could we make this money? We were hot, sweaty, exhausted, and broke. But hey, we looked amazing in our scantily clad dance gear, showing off our well exercised bodies.

Then Lisa said, *look at you guys. You should do a drag show at Connie's.*

Lisa was referring to Connections, the gay nightclub in Northbridge. We all stopped and looked at her. It was a wickedly brilliant idea. Lisa had framed our greatest impact within the context of what an audience wanted. She'd married our performance with the change an audience was seeking – outrageously camp entertainment that paid homage to and celebrated the gay community. We had found the brand truth for that moment.

It was my job to sell the story to the manager at Connie's. I dropped by early that night and nervously stumbled through my pitch.

You had me at drag show. The manager could smell money and he laid down the terms – *we'll do a $20 cover charge after 11 pm. You boys come on at midnight and strut your stuff. We'll split the door takings 50/50. If you draw a good crowd on your first Saturday night, we'll run it again the next Saturday.*

All I could think of was 1800 people times $10 equals $18K. But the club couldn't hold 1800 people. It was probably lucky to hold 400, so how would that work?

I had no idea if it was a good deal or not. But we were out of options. We might still need to bake a few cakes, but this would surely put a dent in the fund-raising target. It was time to create the show.

You can't half do drag. You must fully commit, or you come out looking a complete arse. Commitment for me meant learning to walk in heels. The girls had found a pair of boots for me that left no questions about the persona required to do them justice. Talk about learning to walk in their shoes. The strut I developed, with a matching attitude, was hip-dislocatingly dangerous. I was in my element!

I want to pause for a moment and make a point. Reflect again on the two questions to ask to discover your truth:

- What's the greatest impact we can make on our audience?

- What's the greatest impact our audience seeks?

Think of these questions the way a basketballer uses their feet to pivot. The answer to the first question is your pivot foot. This is your shoe of self or organisational truth and must stay firmly planted on the ground. It's the essence of who you are and what makes your brand remarkable. If this anchor foot detaches from the ground, you start to drift aimlessly. The other foot is your audience shoe; it may move around until you land on an audience that highly values your impact.

In the case of this story, our pivot foot was our ability to entertain a crowd with song and dance. Our other foot had landed on an audience who highly valued this impact. Back to the story ...

Saturday night soon arrived. A few hours before the show, the phone rang at my home. A twangy, nasal English voice spoke. *Hello Tim? It's Danny La Rue.*

Someone was playing a gag, right? Danny La Rue was a world-famous female impersonator. I first heard his name growing up because my brothers would say *I need a Danny La Rue* as rhyming slang while making a B-line for the toilet.

I dismissed it. *Yeah right, piss off, who is this?*

The voice was unperturbed. *Tim, Nigel gave me your number. I'd love to come and see your show tonight.*

Oh my god. Nigel, one of our lecturers at uni – yes, my dear friend who had helped me so much. I could almost hear his laughter from the neighbouring suburb. Nigel loved the shock factor that his little black book of seemingly endless famous performers could produce on his students. This was the real deal.

Any chance of a table for two near the stage, dear?

I was buzzing. I didn't know who to call first – my fellow performers to give them the goss, or my brothers to tell them *I'm going to have a Danny La Rue*. This was getting more bizarre by the moment.

The girls had worked the marketing beat in the week leading up to the show. As we walked onto the stage at midnight, it felt like every gay man in Perth had turned up. People were quite literally standing on the bar and hanging from the rafters. The show itself wouldn't have won any awards, I promise you, but that was nothing six brave lads in fishnets and crop tops couldn't fix. The crowd went wild. We had pulled it off.

For the record, I didn't mention to Danny what his name was synonymous with in my family. He was far too gracious, humble, and gentlemanly to bring the tone down to my level.

There's nothing quite like a nightclub the morning after. I walked alone into what felt like a scene from a gangster movie – I was here to collect the cash. With every step my soles peeled off the sticky, pungent floor, breaking the silence and announcing my arrival.

I found the manager at the end of a long dark hall, sitting in his office behind a large mahogany desk, upon which sat a shopping bag full of cash.

Well done lad, 415 people. That's $4150 in cash for you and your troupe. Let's do it all again next week, hey?

And that we did. In the end we did the show three Saturday nights running and raised nearly $17,000 … beats baking!

In business, your truth is your greatest friend. When you present your truth in the context of the impact your audience seeks, you transform the perception of your value.

It's time to discover your brand truth.

Workbook Exercise 3:

Define your brand truth

Firstly, divide your target audience into two segments – current users and potential new users. So now there are two factors at play – why do people buy your product or service in the first place, and then why do they come back? Current and potential new users are both very important but may have different needs.

For this exercise I want you to imagine your brand as a shop on a typical retail shopping strip. Your shop has two doors – a front door that all new users walk through, and a side entrance where current users and referrals re-enter. Along the strip are all your competitors, also with shop fronts.

Now let's add the protagonist to this story. Walking along this shopping strip, heading for your main competitor, is your audience Avatar – your potential new user. But to get to the competitor they first need to walk past your door. Hanging above your front door is shingle that says:

"We promise to …"

Here's the question – what does the rest of your shingle say? What are the few words etched on your shingle after, "We promise to …" that cut to the heart of your Avatar's greatest want, that your brand can give them? What will stop them in their tracks and make them compelled to enter your shop?

Write down all the potential promises – think about what your audience Avatar urgently wants and what's stopping them from getting it. Look back at your answers to Exercise 1 when you revealed what they really want. As you ponder your promises and try to find the apex of impact and desire, consider you've got less than a second to capture your Avatar's attention. Make sure those few words punch hard.

"We promise to [insert your brand truth]."

When given the option of simple or complex, people will nearly always choose simple. Therefore, it's far more effective to start with the conversation the customer is already having in their own head. Make it easy for them to want to engage with you. As Peter Drucker, the great business thinker of the early 20th century, said: *you can't sell anything to anyone until you understand their problem.*

Now do the same exercise for the shingle above the side door for current users. It's possible the reason someone buys from you initially is very different to the reason they come back. Perhaps once they're on the inside you take them on a far greater journey. But if you don't get them in the door in the first place, you'll never have this opportunity.

Here are examples of brand truths from three of the case studies we've looked at already:

> Imaginarium: We promise to make play an essential part of children's development.
>
> St John Ambulance Victoria: We promise to deliver first-aid that saves lives.
>
> Red Nose: We promise to create a future where no child dies suddenly or unexpectedly.

The truth is the kernel, not the story. You're not trying to write an ad slogan here. Remove the marketing lens and seek the simple truth. It's an internal statement that will inform your brand story. When you find your brand truth, the resulting impact on your business is like a halo over your brand ... or, in the case of Krispy Kreme, an original glazed doughnut.

We're not selling doughnuts, people

The first Krispy Kreme doughnut store to open outside the USA was in Penrith, Sydney in 2003. It was off the back of years of hype around the mystique of these great-tasting doughnuts. It was the brand truth for Krispy Kreme that triggered a story and experiences that made the Sydney launch of Krispy Kreme completely wild.

Krispy Kreme had identified years earlier that the biggest impact they could have on their audience was to make someone a hero by being the bearer of gifts in the form of a dozen original-glazed doughnuts. The biggest emotional impact the audience wanted, although they'd never say it, was to be seen as a hero by their peers or friends or family.

This was the brand truth of Krispy Kreme – the intersection between their greatest impact and the greatest desire of the audience: *we'll make you a hero.*

I joined the Krispy Kreme marketing team as attention turned to the national brand rollout.

The truth, *we'll make you a hero*, dictated the entire strategy. Every *story* we created was about making people heroes by presenting the Krispy Kreme brand in the context of the change the audience was seeking. But here's the crazy part – aside from as much product as we wanted, we had zero dollars to do it. Before the Penrith store first opened, the company gave away 300,000 doughnuts to create these hero experiences.

In morning rush hour, we would literally pull the vintage Krispy Kreme van onto the kerb in the CBD and swing open the back doors. A small bag of doughnuts does not make you a hero. Walking into work with a big flat box of one dozen freshly made doughnuts elevates you to legend status. So that's what we did. We'd give away hundreds of dozens of boxes to city workers passing by. Then we'd vanish as quickly as we came. We targeted creative and design agencies, media outlets, and radio broadcasters live on air. We plied Virgin hosties with dozens upon dozens of doughnuts to share with outbound passengers. The stories people began to tell about sharing a dozen Krispy Kremes with colleagues and friends became renowned.

We weren't selling doughnuts. We were selling the opportunity to be a hero, in the form of a box of one dozen original-glazed to share with friends.

Key chapter takeaways

- Structure your thinking for Your Amazing Brand Story using the proven formula: Truth + Story + Experience = Impact.

- Know precisely who your target audience is and why.

- The greatest impact you can make is often the essence of who you are and what makes you unique.

- The point at which your brand can impact your audience's greatest emotional need is your brand truth.

- Finding your brand truth is the kernel for your story, not the story itself (the marketing polish comes later).

CHAPTER THREE

Everyone wants to be better

so give them what they want

like only your brand can give it.

Give them stories they will share

and the experiences they seek to live it.

Now add a good splash of emotion

The role of your brand is to add emotion to your truth. The simplest way to create this is for your brand to have an opinion, belief or attitude.

Does a coffee snob want a cup of coffee? No – they want an experience from people who understand what it takes to create a sublime caffeine hit. That's the difference. That's the *experience* the coffee snob is searching for, and they will walk past any number of cafés to buy from a brand that gives it to them.

Herein lies the secret to commercially successful stories. When you bring your truth to life for your audience in the context of your brand's emotions, you separate your offer from the pack – you become distinctive and perhaps incomparable.

That's what we're going to do in this chapter – first we'll explore the power of layering brand emotions over your truth by looking at how some of the best brands (both large and small) do it, then I'll walk you through an exercise to discover the best emotions to use to breathe life into your brand.

The rebel

Phil Knight, the co-founder of Nike, famously once said he hates advertising. Dan Wieden, Co-Founder of Wieden+Kennedy, Nike's ad agency since 1982, clarified this further when he said, *Phil Knight didn't want to sell you something – he wanted to help you be something.*

At the time, Phil was breaking the mould. Today, that's what good brands do – help their audience be better.

When I joined Nike in 2005, we had a goal – to be the number one technical running shoe brand in Australia (running shoes that runners wore as opposed to sports fashion shoes). The Nike brand DNA is anchored in running shoes. *By runners, for runners* was the way Nike positioned itself in the early days of the company.

Back in 2005 we were tracking a little behind in sales to both Brooks and New Balance. But we were getting our butts handed to us on a plate by ASICS. Nike had 14% market share of technical running shoes. ASICS had 44%.

There's nothing like a challenge.

To turn the tide, it was clear we had to think differently. Normal was not going to cut the mustard. As always, the truth resides with the consumer – in this case, runners (elite runners especially) were telling us they wanted more from their running experience. There had not been a significant change in the sport for decades. Everything was telling us it was time.

Nike Running's brand truth was to *ignite runners to energise and change the sport forever*. That's what they wanted and that's what we believed Nike could give them.

At its core, the most powerful emotion that Nike can give its audience is to be a rebel. The brand was born rebellious. The best Nike athletes are born rebels. When Nike innovates and inspires with a spirit of rebellion, people respond.

A 30-point gap in market share demanded a plan like no other. Pretty ads and clever headlines weren't going to shift the needle. It was time to be rebellious.

One of the best marketers I've worked with (an innate rebel himself and a very dear friend), Michael Scott, led the brand planning process. Scottie's ability to see the bigger picture and sniff out opportunity is spellbinding.

The foundation of our plan was anchored in the insight that experiencing Nike's running product was the most effective way to change perceptions. We knew when the right Nike shoe was fitted, the running experience matched or exceeded every other brand. The key was to get them on the feet of the people who could influence others, and to do it in a rebellious way.

So that's exactly what we did.

We identified Australia's 5,000 most influential people within the running community, then fitted and educated them in the right Nike running shoe. Podiatrists, physios, personal trainers, and staff in running specialty stores.

Every influencer was given access to an exclusive purchase program so they could buy Nike running shoes and gear for themselves and their family at cost.

We did the same in secondary schools across the country – we pitted school against school in a total kilometres run event called the Nike+ Schools Challenge. Every runner was fitted with Nike running shoes at cost.

We created Nike Run Clubs around the county, each one with a shoe amnesty. You can run in whatever brand of shoes you like, but if you throw your ASICS, New Balance or Brooks in the big recycling cage, we'll fit you in a pair of new Nike running shoes at cost.

Runners responded and the cages overflowed.

All this coincided with Nike releasing amazing product innovations, particularly Nike Free Run, which had captured a subculture of barefoot running devotees and was going mainstream in a hurry. Plus, Nike's partnership with Apple now meant music, running and social media were blurring.

The planets were beginning to align, and the pendulum started to swing. Brand-tracking research and in-store sales told us we were onto something. We put the foot to the floor.

Retail floor staff remained the biggest untapped influencers. Thousands of twenty-ish-year-olds, working in the hundreds of sporting goods retailers around the country (Foot Locker, Rebel Sport and The Athlete's Foot) hold a lot of power in the advice they dish out. They are smart, sporty people, usually working part-time while studying at university. In short, they love sport, are switched on, and live for a party.

With these insights we launched an experience called Nikeology, a digital information and inspiration platform. In five-minute slots the retail floor staff could learn about Nike running shoes; if they got the short quiz right, they earnt points to score an invite to the mother of all Nike parties with an A-list of athletes.

In year one, the take up of Nikeology was ho-hum. Even so, we partied with 500 retail floor staff across three locations around the country. The story of the party spread. Footage emerged of Roger Federer in a warehouse playing table tennis against Rebel, Foot Locker and The Athlete's Foot retail floor staff. Roger took it easy until he looked like losing, then he shed his jacket and blew the roof off the joint. It didn't hurt that three weeks later he won the Australian Open.

Nikeology was the story retail floor staff were talking about.

In year two, Nikeology went bonkers. Roger came to the party, won table tennis, and then won the Australian Open … again. His winning ways were rubbing off on us. At the same time, we were closing the sales gap. We passed New Balance and Brooks, and the puff of dust on the horizon was ASICS.

The Nike Run Clubs (NRC) were proving to be a powerful consumer experience. They were dominated by women hanging out after work and running the pants off our run leaders. These women told us they liked NRC – they could catch up with girlfriends and run together because they didn't feel safe running by themselves, especially at night.

Bingo: we'd found another story.

The truth: *Women can't run wherever and whenever they want. They are restricted by fear. They are restricted by the night.*

Then came the task of layering the Nike brand emotion on this truth. How could we help young female runners be rebellious?

What if they took a stand against the fear imposed upon them to run at night?

That's when *She Runs the Night* was born:

> *We are the rule-breakers. The renegades. The troublemakers. We're here to start a revolution. You say it's not safe to run after dark. We make the rules around here. We'll run at midnight. We'll run until the sun comes up. And then we'll start again.*

> *You draw the line and we'll cross it. There's only one thing to be afraid of tonight. Us. Tonight we defy the darkness. Tonight we make a stand. Tonight we race.*

This *brand story* became our compass. It informed all the experiences we created – midnight training runs, event T-shirts, bespoke *She Runs* running shoes, digital experiences and the *She Runs The Night* race through Sydney.

I still get goosebumps listening to women recount their experience of the lead-up to the event and the night itself – the incredible lighting on the course, the bands around every corner and the party on the finish line. Our agencies won lots of awards, but it's the small difference it made in women's lives that mattered most.

We helped them make a statement, if only just for one night. We backed it up the following year and double the number of women took part.

One event rarely changes a culture. Sadly, the same fear imposed on women is as true today as it was then. It will be the sum of the parts that forges any lasting change. But it's my belief that helping people and brands make a difference, by creating amazing stories and experiences – will make the world a better place. That's my truth. It's why I do what I do.

In 2013, one year after the first *She Runs The Night* experience and eight years after the journey started, Nike overtook ASICS and claimed the number one position in sales of technical running shoes. An incredible company-wide achievement. And yes, the entire team partied on the finish line.

The cost of not knowing what you stand for

A crystal-clear brand story enables people to project outcomes. *If I buy brand X, I'm more likely to feel Y.* The decision to purchase is based on the anticipated payoff.

Your audience's belief that your brand can give them that pay-off is directly connected to the margin you make. The greater the need, and the greater the belief you can deliver it, the more you can charge.

In other words, when you frame your impact in the context of the emotional change your audience seeks, you transform your value.

Consider this:

- A Gillette razor gives you the confidence to look your best.

- Handee Ultra paper towels make you a whiz in the kitchen.

- Swisse supplements make you feel younger and more vital.

- A CPA certified accountant instils you with trust that you're working with the best.

All these brands invest in controlling the emotion attached to the brand. Why? Because owning the emotional solution positions these brands as the change their audience seeks, and therefore delivers both an emotional outcome and commercial margin by the truckload.

The purpose of marketing is to establish an emotional connection to your product or service, to better enable the sale. Choosing the frame of reference in which your product or service is presented is the simplest way to strike an emotional chord with your audience.

The biggest cost to discovering your brand truth and framing it in the context of the change your audience seeks is your time and energy. The cost of doing nothing is money.

Layering emotions over your truth will mean standing out and being different, just like Imaginarium did with their little door of magic.

Here's another example – this time a smaller brand.

La vie lente

It's French for *the slow life*. Its truth lives in the cute little walled village of Dinan, in the northwest of France. The medieval town dates to the 12th century; the steep, narrow cobblestone streets wind curiously through half-timber, half-stone dwellings and shops. At the base of the village the River Rance gently idles by. Long ago, the river carried supplies of meat, seafood, wine, cheese and fresh goods from the riches of surrounding Brittany. It was an ideal town for Emma and me to meet my folks who were holidaying in Europe.

Everything about Dinan hails back to a simpler time. The roads are too narrow for cars and too steep for bikes, so you join the locals each morning and trudge slowly up the hill to get a fresh baguette from the bakery.

On our final evening the four of us found ourselves at a modest little local restaurant in the middle of town. The waiter greeted us with menus, then explained cuisine toi-même – which, after a game of French charades, we worked out meant 'cook yourself'.

We looked at each other blankly, then at the surrounding tables where indeed the other patrons were *cuisine toi-même-ing*. Okay, when in Dinan …

We ordered what we hoped was an enticing spread of local produce, then waited anxiously for their next move, like a game of chess.

They moved our king into check, in the form of a red-hot stone the shape and size of a chopping board surrounded by the most glorious array of fresh meat, seafood and sauces laid out in the centre of our table. *Bon appetit,* they said.

And *bon appetit* we did. The theatre of cooking the food together was intoxicating. The sizzles and waves of aroma from the scolding stone were sublime. The cooking ritual was a metaphor for the simplicity of life in Dinan – their *brand truth*. Their story was laid out before us on a wooden table – slow down and enjoy what each moment has to offer. The experience was mesmerising.

The waiter had warned us not to put pepper on the stone – not sure why. Later in the evening, as the local pinot did its work, we found out. The temptation was obviously too much for someone as a coughing waft of invisible air filled the room, and we soon found ourselves sipping wine outside on the quaint street while the peppery air disbursed. It didn't matter – we were now under the spell of the slow life, and we all had a story to share.

The scale of your ability to connect with those who matter is limited only by your imagination.

It's time to stand out

Humans have survived and evolved by blending in. As a species, we didn't go to the edge of the forest and yell at the wild beasts on the savannah. We learnt to hide, to be inconspicuous. We learnt not to be different because standing out meant death.

For brands and leaders, the rules are different. Being brave enough to stand up and stand out is rewarded.

Few brands stand out because the deeply ingrained thinking and behaviour is to look like you belong in your business category. For this reason, most industries become a homogeneous wash of similar brands, unconsciously trying to look like each other. That's why real estate agents all look the same. Accountants look the same. Butchers, doctors, lawyers, plumbers … you get the idea. Same, same, same.

But when a sugary carbonated drink appeared that didn't look or act like all the other players in the category, we all took notice. The product tastes like medicine, is packaged in a small medicinal sized can and has apparent magic medicinal qualities that gives you *wings* – the young, and young at heart, went gaga for Red Bull.

A lesson in *truth*, *story* and *experience* for all of us.

Don't compromise your chutzpah. When you do, you dilute your potency, your difference, and your story's potential to deliver the feelings and emotions your audience seeks.

A mother's truth

I suspect my mother never had a Red Bull – shame, the result would have been hilarious.

Mum was a straight shooter. The veneer of niceties and falsehoods annoyed her. She would tell it like it is and deeply value others who did the same. People loved her for her frankness and bold honesty. She didn't need a fizzy drink to grow wings.

Mum's preferred potion was a glass of red wine – after her first sip most evenings, she'd proclaim with a ritual sigh, *ahhh… mothers' milk*. As the years went by, Emma and I loved visiting Mum and Dad, with a bottle or two of special red wine to share over a weekend at their beachside home.

When Mum was diagnosed with Alzheimer's in her early seventies, we all knew the truth according to Jenny Wood was going to get a lot more airtime.

On one of our visits to see the folks, Dad took Emma and me aside and pointed out that a glass or two of wine seemed to be exacerbating the effects of Mum's dementia. She'd become confused and agitated. We were in a bind – the thought of taking Mum's simple pleasure away from her was heart-breaking, but the side effects were clearly distressing her.

Emma, being Emma, researched the topic that afternoon and came back with the lovely idea of adding a little water to Mum's red wine without her knowing – the theory being Mum gets to enjoy a drink with everyone but hopefully without the troubled confusion that too much alcohol induces. So that night we gave it a go.

It worked a treat. We all enjoyed a delicious drop; Mum didn't get too confused, and we had a wonderful evening together. Everyone was happy. We drove back to Melbourne the next day, quietly chuffed that we'd helped the folks in some small way.

Dad later told me that at wine o'clock on the day we'd left, he asked the usual question of Mum – *the bar's open darling, would you like a glass of red?*

To which Mum replied, *yes please dear, but not that shit that Tim and Emma brought down, it was bloody awful.*

Depriving your brand story of its potential is like diluting a good wine. The result will always be a compromised outcome for your audience and for you. Remember: you know the truth and you know the feelings your audience wants, so give it to them at full throttle via your brand. Let them bask in your passionate belief of the uncompromising excellence you deliver. Be a leader in what you do. Be fearless in the knowledge that you will attract those people you want, and repel those you don't.

You don't want to impact everybody – just those who matter to you.

Standing out means impacting the truth

What would your target audience need to believe to buy from you? What would need to happen for them to engage in the products or services you sell?

When people make choices, they buy the solution that delivers the biggest change they desire. It's rarely functional and usually intangible – a feeling that they're not even conscious of.

The opportunity you have is to package the solution they seek in the context of your brand emotions – your competitive advantage. Because at the end of the day, in the moment of truth, that's what matters most. The brand that can best deliver the impact their audience seeks will be the one that gets the sale, again and again.

The children's entertainment group, The Wiggles, is a great example of a brand that does this. The truth of The Wiggles brand lives in the harmony created for both their audiences – child and parent. The child wants to be entertained. The parent, while they'd rarely admit it, wants a guilt-free way to occupy their child – the emotion is entertainment that educates.

The Wiggles coined the phrase *Edutainment* because that's what they give their audience. Edutainment is true to The Wiggles' roots as both trained early childhood educators and rock 'n' rollers. It comes to life in the experiences they create. They position their brand brilliantly for 'the sale' by giving both parent and child the change they seek.

A good barometer of brand strength is the number of third parties that will pay money to associate themselves with a brand (emotional leverage – a.k.a. sponsorship). Our company was fortunate enough to represent The Wiggles for twenty years as their commercial partnership's agency. Finding commercial partners for The Wiggles was easier than most for one reason – emotional brand leadership. The Wiggles were top of the pops during our time together as the most successful preschool brand for corporate partnerships globally.

Money follows impact.

Character is everything

A brand is most simply defined as a *gut feeling* evoked by the mere hint of an organisation or its products or services. When a meaningful impact is made on an audience, people will attribute the feelings evoked by that impact to the brand that made it.

This came to life for me one day when wandering through downtown Chicago, Illinois. I happened across an exhibition of beautifully crafted 18-inch dolls. Each doll was a young girl taking on the world: firefighters, doctors, scientists, athletes, academics, tradies and explorers. Each one had their own mini street window. Inside, I discovered even more dolls. This was girl heaven; a gallery where the hushed tones of mothers and daughters paid respect to the creativity and cultural importance of what was around them. Each doll had its own story about what it contributed to the world.

It was a statement, and it was inspiring.

I walked out a little unsure of what I had just experienced, then saw the sign above the door that read *American Girl*. I was clearly missing something so ventured back in – this time I noticed a staircase.

What was at the top of the stairs blew me away: a grand, five-star café, with white-gloved waiters, was full of over a hundred girls and their mothers having high tea; scones, pancakes, teapots and lattes. At the end of each white-starched tablecloth was a beautifully crafted wooden doll's seat, like a clip-on baby chair but smaller. And in each doll's chair sat the child's own doll, just like the ones I'd seen downstairs. Each doll had a doll's cup and real food: mini cookies and a frothy dolly-chino. My heart melted.

Welcome to American Girl, where *character is everything*. Their brand truth is *the belief in being a trusted partner for parents who want to raise strong, confident girls.*

That's the intangible outcome American Girl projects. And American mothers were paying handsomely for the privilege to be part of it.

When you choose the frame of reference for your product or service, its value is transformed. American Girl, which is owned by the toy maker Mattel, choose to present their products in the context of an art gallery. Refined, sophisticated and distinguished. That's the story they tell; therefore, that's what their audience feels.

It's time to dial up the emotional splendour of Your Amazing Brand Story by creating your emotional brand description – a short sentence that cuts to the heart of what your brand stands for.

Workbook Exercise 4:

Layer on your brand emotions

Ask yourself: what does your audience want to *feel* when they interact with your brand and how does your brand create that feeling? To answer this question, insert the right words for your brand into your emotional brand description:

'We make [insert audience Avatar] feel [insert word/s] through a sense of [insert word/s]'.

Here are some indicative examples of emotional brand descriptions from brands we've looked at so far:

> McDonald's: We make *families* feel *rewarded and connected* through a sense of *fun*.

> Nike: We make *athletes* feel *inspired* through a sense of *rebellion*.

> American Girl: We make *girls* feel *joyous* through a sense of *adventure and empowerment*.

> Red Nose: We make *new parents* feel *safer* through a sense of *knowledge and care*.

> The Wiggles: We make *young families* feel *smarter* through a sense of *playful fun*.

Word prompts

Use these word prompts to help discover the right words for your brand, or come up with your own words:

> Smart, connected, grounded, healed, safe, understood, beautiful, natural, healthy, handy, comfortable, indulged, adventurous, wise, prestigious, fabulous, special, needed, crafty, athletic, progressive, diverse, innovative, sensual, important, rebellious, mystical, informed, influential, brave, playful, optimistic, joyful, funny, cared for, refined, articulate, daring, provocative, knowledgeable, fearless, excited.

Later you'll use your emotional brand description to add power to your story, but for the moment focus on uncovering the right words. Walk in the shoes of your audience and craft and refine your words until they're as compelling and authentic as possible.

Good brands walk in the door before you

Moscow in 1990 was a weird place. It was one year after the Berlin Wall had come down and one year before the USSR was to dissolve, marking the end of the Cold War. Gorbachev's Perestroika had done its job.

The city, I discovered back then, had two stories. One was terribly sad as people queued with ticket vouchers to get basic supplies like bread and milk. But there was something else happening just under the surface. Down every grey, oppressed alley and in the back seat of every other run-down cab, the black-market trade was alive. Goods were being exchanged for US dollars. The ruble was like Monopoly money. It was the Soviet youth who seemed energised and renewed.

I walked into a hotel lobby with my mate Bloomy, the same partner in crime who watched me fall through the ceiling a decade later. We were wearing Levi's jeans because we were looking for a reaction.

Sure enough, we got a hit. A wad of US dollars for our jeans. I was almost feeling guilty. Almost. Good thing we came prepared. We had read before we left home that Russian lads go gaga for Levi's. We pulled two used pairs of Levi's from our backpack. It wasn't a hard sell.

We got talking to our new friends. *What's with the Levi's obsession?*

The answer was telling: *a symbol of America. A symbol of freedom.* That's the change these young Russian guys sought, and a pair of Levi's gave it to them.

A good brand walks in the door long before you do. You'll know Your Amazing Brand Story is working when its reputation precedes you.

In the previous chapters you've defined your audience and your brand truth. And in this chapter you've identified the brand emotions you'll layer over your brand truth. Now it's time to bring it together by learning to become a better storyteller.

Key chapter takeaways

- The key purpose of your brand is to add emotion to your product or service.

- When you wrap your truth in brand emotions, you create your competitive advantage.

- The stronger your brand, the more able your audience is to project the outcome they desire.

- Fitting in to your category (looking like you belong) is the opposite of standing out and being noticed.

- The context in which you present your brand determines its value.

CHAPTER FOUR

Everyone wants to be better

so give them what they want

like only your brand can give it.

Give them stories they will share

and the experiences they seek to live it.

Story is a recipe that works

In business as in life, one of the most effective ways to achieve the desired outcome is to take what already works and use it. Stories are a proven way to inject emotion into a moment. The more visceral the story, the more impact you'll make on your audience.

In this chapter you're going to learn the recipe to telling great stories. Then, using your *audience Avatar*, *brand truth* and *emotional brand description* as your ingredients, you will create Your Amazing Brand Story.

The two stories in business

There are two types of stories in business: *storytelling* and *lived experiences*. To be amazing you must do both.

Storytelling is what we all think of when we think about telling stories in business – the words, images and sounds you use to tell the story of your brand. Storytelling is important, but in isolation it won't make your brand amazing.

Lived experiences are the moments you design that enable your audience to *experience* your story in an instant. Lived experiences light the flame for your audience to spread your story, and that's when your brand story becomes amazing. We'll explore lived experiences in the next chapter.

But keep in mind, the goal is not just to tell a story, but to *be the story*.

In a moment I'll walk you through the framework that great storytellers from all walks of life use to tell stories – but first, it's important to know the three golden rules of using stories in business.

The three golden rules of using stories in business

Businesses who have amazing brand stories do three things:

1. They walk in the shoes of their audience.

2. They embrace vulnerability to reveal their story gold.

3. They structure their stories the way the brain wants to experience them.

Let's look at each one.

Golden Rule 1: Walk in the shoes of your audience

The power of stories lives in empathy – an understanding of what it's like to walk in the shoes of your audience. Exploring their hopes, dreams and fears unlocks the truth of the story you tell.

People care about people, not brands. We only begin to care about brands when we see or experience the impact a brand can make on people's lives. That's it – nothing more, nothing less.

Businesses who use stories effectively tell the story of those they impact most. They make their audience the hero – the driving force behind everything the brand does. The story brings to life the change that was sought, the journey to find it and the impact it's had on their lives. Later in this chapter I'll show you several examples of this.

No one cares about what you do. They care about the impact you make on your audience. Walk in their shoes and tell the story of the impact people have experienced.

Golden Rule 2: Embrace vulnerability to reveal your story gold

There's a truth to storytelling that few people recognise; we don't care about other people's success; we care about their failures. Great storytelling occurs when it's humanised – when the flaws in a character are exposed.

When a storyteller reveals their imperfections, they uncover their gold. Within your wonderful flaws and quirks that make you and your brand who you are, you'll discover a wealth of stories anchored in humour and humility. These are often your most loveable characteristics.

What were the challenges you faced in fighting to achieve your goals? Being vulnerable means sometimes you'll share those compromising moments we might normally hide. But sharing these moments opens the doorway to amazing reactions like spontaneity, curiosity, passion, laughter and love. Vulnerability makes audiences stop, listen, care and believe.

We build trust in the storyteller when they're real – when they own their story.

Golden Rule 3: Structure your story the way the brain wants to experience it

Good stories are constructed on a well-established pattern the brain recognises and responds to. Learn the pattern and you'll learn how to connect with your audience.

The brain loves patterns. It's constantly and subconsciously leaping ahead, connecting dots to find patterns and anticipate outcomes. It's how we make sense of the world. Patterns means predictability. Anticipating outcomes is important for each one of us, as it brings familiarity, comfort and security.

It's the very reason children love repetition, because they are patterns.

Why did the chicken cross the road?

Knock knock ...

Once upon a time ...

Each of these lines sparks an anticipation in our brain for what comes next.

Like the pattern of music to a muso, the story pattern gives a structure and scaffold for the storyteller to create and play within. When you hear music that doesn't fit your preferred pattern, it jars ... *not my thing*. The very same is true for storytelling. Knowing the story pattern unlocks the magic.

The art and science of storytelling

Every story begins with a problem – a challenge that a character needs to overcome.

Three little pigs are being chased by a hungry wolf.

Romeo and Juliet are in love, but their families despise each other.

Charlie's family is poor, and he yearns for a better life.

The problem is the catalyst. The fight to overcome the problem is the journey we're taken on. What the character learns from the journey is the change the audience experiences. Bringing all this together in a story is a collision of art and science. I'll demonstrate …

> It was another one of those nights. I needed to sleep but the harder I tried, the more the same thoughts kept tumbling through my head.

This time it was work on my mind. My new job had put me on the steepest learning curve of my marketing career. Without question, I was out of my depth, but the people around me were unbelievably talented and supportive, and the opportunities being thrown my way were humbling. So, I lay in bed trying to solve problems I had no idea how to solve.

Ridiculous o'clock became early morning. In the next room, our two-year-old son Harry lay sleeping. Emma, six months pregnant with our daughter Pippa, was sound asleep next to me.

Then it started to happen. I felt a tightening in my chest. I sat up. Now it was pain. I slid out of bed and found myself on the floor. It was hard to breathe. I woke Emma. I was cold but sweating. I made it to the sofa in the lounge room, and that's the last I can remember.

I could then hear a male voice speaking calmly, but the words weren't calming … *probable cardiac arrest*. I opened my eyes to find a paramedic hovering over me with paddles in his hands. A female voice was calling out numbers with a speed that implied alarm. The gravity of what I was hearing hit me. Emma's voice sounded like it was on a distant radio. I wanted to see her and Harry, one last time. Then everything went dark again.

Later I learnt that my heart rate was dropping under 40 bpm, sending me in and out of consciousness.

Emma, is Tim an elite athlete? It was the male paramedic's voice again. Before Emma could even answer, the female paramedic lifted my shirt and reached her own medical conclusion: *Nope*.

I want to pause the story. What just happened for you then? What happens in the brain when we hear a story? How can you replicate that effect in your business?

Here's a rudimentary science lesson from a guy who dropped all sciences after year ten. At the brain's emotional centre is an almond-shaped lobe called the amygdala. Think of it as the brain's triage unit for emotional responses.

The human brain has evolved to be an energy-conserving machine. That's how the species has survived and thrived. If you don't need to use energy, don't, because later you will, and it could mean the difference between life and death. And so, we've evolved to today where with every incoming impulse, the brain asks three questions and triggers an automatic response depending on the answer:

1. Is this a threat?

2. Is this of interest?

3. Is this boring?

The brain will triage by releasing chemicals to trigger the desired response:

- If it's a threat, the brain releases cortisol (fight or flight)

- If it's of interest or benefit, the brain releases oxytocin (the love drug) or dopamine (the reward drug)

- If it's boring or complicated, the brain conserves energy and tunes out – the mind drifts to thinking of something far less draining.

When we're trying to influence and persuade people, our task as storytellers is to get past the amygdala by releasing the right chemicals in the brain. As the story develops, other chemicals are released. By the end of a good story the brain is swimming in a cocktail of chemicals, evoking a powerful emotional response.

Let's go back to the story before the chemicals in your brain run dry and I lose you. The paramedic had just reached an accurate medical assessment of my not-so-toned midriff…

> I sat up. The paddles were set aside. I felt the squeeze of Emma's hand – she was incredibly calm, which I remember thinking was amazing given she lost her father from a heart attack when she was only eleven years old.
>
> Strapped in the ambulance trolley, I had the inglorious procession past the awaiting throng of dressing gown clad neighbours. I think we all realised I would be okay when I asked the ambo if we could do lights and sirens to the hospital. He knocked me back – where was his sense of occasion?
>
> Staring at the ceiling in a hospital has a way of bringing the unadulterated truth to the surface.

A perspective that only a seemingly near-death moment can bring. Later that day the cardiologist returned to my room after having conducted what felt like more tests than I'd had sleepless nights. My heart was perfectly fine. He told me I most likely had a severe anxiety attack. Then he said the phrase that has stuck with me since.

Less head, more heart.

He suggested I spend less time thinking and worrying, and more time doing and enjoying. *The world is at your feet, young man, get on with living.* When you know what is right in your heart, get on and do it; embrace it with all of yourself and enjoy the journey that follows.

We all need a pep talk occasionally – or in this case, a gentle dressing down. Just like Jerry back in London on that cold winter's night when he told me I was going about job-hunting the wrong way. The cardiologist was right.

Stories in business work exactly that same way as the structure of this story. They begin with a problem your audience wants to overcome – the change they seek. We then go on the journey to understand their fight to overcome it. And finally, we experience how the journey changed them.

The story is in the struggle, not the victory. The beginning and end phases of a story are bookends to the main game.

The Square Root of Story

Every story has three district phases – a beginning, a middle and an end. In business we call them *the problem, the fight,* and *the change.*

If we were to chart the emotional journey of my anxiety attack, the story arc dictated by the problem, the fight, and the change would look like the square root symbol. This is the structure the brain recognises – the pattern. I call it *The Square Root of Story.*

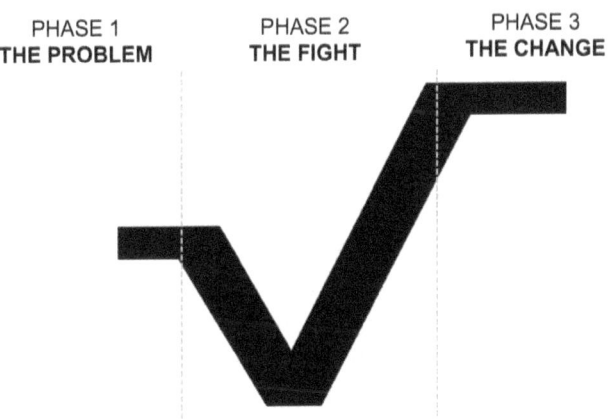

The *problem* was I thought I was having a heart attack.

The *fight* was the journey my mind, body and family went on.

The *change* was my altered perspective on life.

Speech writers, novelists, script writers, creative agencies: the best storytellers in the world use this structure. All the stories I've told in this book adhere to this same structure. Why? Because this is the structure that connects the head with the heart in a listener. A clear brand story told this way is the Trojan Horse for successful business. It's the vehicle that enables a brand to emotionally engage with its audience.

Each phase of The Square Root of Story has a role. Our clients tell us that understanding the role of each phase and visualising *The Square Root of Story* helps them write and tell their own Amazing Brand Story.

Here's how it works.

Every story centres on a hero – a central character whose journey the audience follows through The Square Root of Story. In each phase the audience must care about the hero and what happens next to trigger the release of the right chemicals into the brain. You know that euphoric feeling you have at the end of a good movie? That's the result of riding the rollercoaster of The Square Root of Story.

- The Problem: we meet the hero and understand what's important to them, what they value and what's at stake – empathy is established and oxytocin is released. Then something happens in the hero's world – life cannot go on as it was and The Square Root journey suddenly heads south. We're invested and want to know more.

- The Fight: the hero faces choices and obstacles. They battle with different alternatives, failing each time as The Square Root Journey bottoms out. Then the hero finds a new path, a potential way through, and The Square Root Journey turns and begins its climb. Here comes the dopamine – the feeling that a reward is at hand.

- The Change: the hero's experience has changed them. They have a new, elevated perspective. Life didn't perhaps go the way they'd planned but consequently, their world view has changed. The full cocktail is now doing its work and the audience feels fulfilled.

Most stories also have what I call a guide. The guide usually appears (but not always) at the lowest point of The Square Root of Story to help the hero. The guide is what Dumbledore is to Harry Potter; Mary Poppins to Mr Banks; Yoda to Luke.

Pick any commercially successful feature film and you'll see The Square Root of Story in action. How about Academy Award winning film *The King's Speech*?

The King's Speech, Phase 1: The Problem

We meet Prince Albert, Duke of York (the hero) and second in line to the throne. He's afflicted by a terrible stutter which is devastating for him. We see his struggle and the pain it causes. Then in quick succession, his father the King dies and his elder brother King Edward VIII abdicates the throne. A stuttering King George is reluctantly thrust into the spotlight.

The connection with the audience is established first, then there's an event and the Square Root Journey heads down.

The King's Speech, Phase 2: The Fight

This is no ordinary time in history. World War II has broken out and the Commonwealth needs a voice, but the King doesn't have one. He tries everything but without success. In a desperate attempt to find a solution, the Queen finds an unorthodox Australian speech specialist in London (the guide). At first the King resists the attempts by the specialist to connect at a deeper level – a struggle for a man of his upbringing. But with time and dedication the King begins to soften, and in turn, slowly finds his voice.

The journey continues down as we experience the challenges until it bottoms out; then, with a new approach and the introduction of a guide, it starts heading up.

The King's Speech, Phase 3: The Change

At a time when his people need him most, the King must speak live on radio to the world. With his speech specialist by his side, the King delivers one of the great speeches of his time. In addressing his stutter, the King has also addressed his ability to connect deeply with others. A deep bond is formed between the King and his specialist that lasts for the rest of their lives. This is actually a story of friendship. That's its truth. The King's perspectives have changed.

The Square Root Journey rises above its initial starting point and remains elevated. The hero character and the audience walk away with their worldview altered.

The trap most brands fall for

Here's the trick: most brands fall for the trap of telling a story from their own perspective, thinking they are the hero. Your brand story is not about your brand. It's about the people your brand impacts – the scenarios they faced, the choices they made and the journey they went on.

Effective storytelling in business uses the audience as the hero, and brings their journey to life, then positions the brand as the guide. Your audience is Luke. Your brand is Yoda.

What the audience wants is the *feeling* the brand's product or service will give them. They get this by seeing others experience it.

NOTE: When telling your own story, as opposed to a brand's, there's one big exception: you become the hero. There may or may not be a guide, but the same rules apply:

1. Walk in the shoes of your audience.

2. Embrace vulnerability to reveal your story gold.

3. Structure the story the way the brain wants to experience it.

Workbook Exercise #5:

Write Your Amazing Brand Story

The objective of this exercise is to break down and show you how successful brands write their Amazing Brand Story so you can create yours. Amazing brands do three things to bring their story to life:

1. Create a crystal-clear brand statement.

    These are the words (often the brand's strapline) that immediately resonate with what the audience wants.

2. Write a succinct synopsis of the brand story.

   This is a concise version of your story used to inform and inspire storytelling (words and visuals) across all your audience touchpoints.

3. Bring the brand story to life the way their audience wants to experience it.

   This is your brand story in all its glory – full of emotion, colour, sounds and life.

Let's work through each one and look at examples so you can create Your Amazing Brand Story.

Step 1: Create a crystal-clear brand statement

This short statement (usually no more the half a dozen words) tells your audience exactly what it is you want to be known for. Like the point of an arrow, its purpose is to penetrate the heart and mind of your target audience immediately.

You've already done the hard work of assembling the components for this; it's now a matter of interpreting the words in a concise way for your audience.

To do this, express the essence of your brand truth with the feeling of your emotional brand statement, as a succinct phrase.

Here are examples of how some of the brands we've looked at do this.

Nike:

Brand Truth:	**Emotional brand description:**
We promise to bring inspiration and innovation to every athlete in the world.	We make athletes feel inspired through a sense of rebellion.

Brand statement:

Just do it.

McDonald's:

Brand Truth:	**Emotional brand description:**
We promise to reward you.	We make people feel connected through a sense of fun.

Brand statement:

I'm lovin' it.

Red Nose

Brand Truth:	**Emotional brand description:**
We promise to create a future where no child dies suddenly or unexpectedly.	We make new parents feel safe through knowledge and care.

Brand statement:

Saving little lives.

Your turn: looking at your brand truth next to your emotional brand description, create your brand statement.

Step 2: Write a synopsis of your brand story

To write your brand story synopsis, you're going to use exactly the same structure as I've used to write every story in this book, and exactly the same structure as the best brands in the world use to create their brand stories: The Square Root of Story.

Write three short paragraphs under each of the following headings:

> The Problem: The context of your audience Avatar in the moment immediately before they discovered your brand and the problem they were experiencing.
>
> The Fight: What they did about the problem, their reaction, and their struggle.
>
> The Change: The solution they found (your brand), how it made them feel and their altered perspective at the end of it all.

As you write the synopsis of your brand story, use your Audience Avatar information, your brand truth and your emotional brand description to inform your story. Remember to walk in the shoes of the audience, embrace the vulnerability and tell the story through their eyes.

Here's an indicative example to help you see how it could be expressed. Note: these are my words and not used or approved by Red Nose.

Red Nose

Audience Avatar: new mother

The problem: Four days after our first baby was born, we arrived home, and pretty soon we realised we actually had no idea what we were doing. We didn't know how to make safer choices for our precious child. I started to stress out.

The fight: We searched the internet and asked friends and family how to make the right choices – how to get our baby to sleep safely, what products to use, how to use them – but the messages were all mixed. We got different advice on nearly everything. We were now totally confused.

The change: Then we found Red Nose – it was like a light was switched on for us. Everything they shared with us was evidence-based with practical advice to use immediately. Within a day we knew how to choose safer baby products, put them in safer places for our child and use safer baby practices. I even got my mum and dad to do the course. The people at Red Nose were incredible. It's such peace of mind knowing we're doing all we can to protect our beautiful baby.

To help in the writing process we've created a handy one-page Square Root of Story writer's guide you can print out and follow. Download here:

YourAmazingBrandStory.com/toolkit

Step 3: Bring Your Amazing Brand Story to life the way your audience wants to experience it

Now it's time to get really inspired by looking at the work of some of the best creative minds in the world. Watch the collection of brand story video examples in the toolkit link below. Plot The Square Root of Story journey in each. Seeing how others do it will inspire you to bring your own Amazing Brand Story to life.

YourAmazingBrandStory.com/toolkit

Key chapter takeaways

- There are two types of stories in business – storytelling and lived experiences. To be amazing you need to do both.

- The three golden rules of using stories in business are:

  1. Walk in the shoes of your audience

  2. Embrace vulnerability to reveal your story 'gold'

  3. Structure your story the way the brain wants to experience it.

- Your brand story is not about your brand – it's about the people your brand impacts.

- The Square Root of Story provides the proven story arc that will engage your audience.

CHAPTER FIVE

Everyone wants to be better

so give them what they want

like only your brand can give it.

Give them stories they will share

and the experiences they seek to live it.

Experiences are the ultimate form of story

There is nothing as powerful as an experience. An experience has the potential to change lives. Your brand story isn't amazing until it's experienced. This is the final element of our formula:

Truth + Story + Experiences = Impact

The experiences I'm talking about are the moments when the essence of what you want to be known for, your brand truth, becomes a story your audience experiences. It's like the baton change in a relay race – you create the opportunity for a moment and your audience runs with it.

We call them *lived experiences* and they're important because your brand story is not what you say it is – it's what your audience believes it is.

Remember the little magic door on the streets of Spain, the doll gallery in Chicago, the cook-it-yourself experience in Dinan,

France? They are all examples of lived experiences. It's those moments that made the brand story amazing. Stories influence how your audience feel about you. Lived experiences determine what they believe about you.

However, here's the stark reality – very few companies integrate lived experiences into their business. Organisations will spend tens or hundreds of thousands of dollars to create lovely words and images to adorn their website, office, shop walls, packaging, and advertisements. They feel wonderful for a month or two, but usually very little changes. Words and images are empty without actions.

In this chapter we're going to explore what lived experiences look like and how others have created them. Then in the final workbook exercise I will walk you through our four-step process to creating lived experiences you can integrate into your business.

To create deeper connections with your audience, you must accept your role as creator and conductor of lived experiences. When you transition from simply telling stories to creating lived experiences, your brand becomes the story.

And when you *are* the story, the emotional sparks fly.

The Irish inn

You may have seen the stage musical *Once*. If you haven't, it's a romantic journey that uses an Irish bar as both the set and the metaphor for the show. At its very essence, *Once* is about the power of music to connect us all. Shared music. Music you might hear in an Irish pub. Music that strokes the soul.

The creative minds behind *Once* are marvellous storytellers but arguably better marketers. They found a way for people to experience their brand in a manner that creates stories every night. I can't hum one song from *Once*, but I can share my story about it.

Usually when you walk into a theatre, you find your seat then wait for the show to start. Perhaps flick through the program, stand up a few times for others as they arrive – you know the drill.

The producers of *Once* turned convention on its head, using the truth of the brand to create a moment.

As Emma and I walked into the auditorium, we could see the inside of an Irish bar on stage. It oozed charm; wood-panelled walls dressed with old photos and hazy mirrors, all intimating hundreds of years of Gaelic happiness. A barman was polishing glasses, and a pianist was settling himself behind a well-loved piano. An usher mentioned to us that we're welcome to grab a beer at the bar and gestured towards the stage.

Huh?

We timidly walked up the steps and joined the other brave souls who had done the same. The piano player, oblivious to his surrounds as seasoned musos seem to be, started tinkling a haunting Irish melody. A woman picked up a fiddle, put a foot on the piano stool and lifted the tempo a notch. Over the next fifteen minutes the pub transformed into a fully-fledged Irish jig. Musos walked from among us – guitars, fiddles, tambourines and drum boxes appeared from nowhere. The Irish folk singing and foot-stamping was raw, spontaneous and totally contagious.

The producers had created a moment. A moment born from the essence of their brand truth – *Music feeds the soul.* They fed everyone's soul and gave us an experience worth spreading.

Lived experiences are social currency. People love sharing their stories of experiences. The opportunity you have is to create lived experiences where stories are born. On the night we saw *Once*, by the time we took our seats our hearts were settled at an Irish Inn.

When you create *lived experiences,* you're baking your truth into your offering that gives your audience a story – now they have an experience to share with others.

The benefit of a good *lived experience* is it changes your brand's status. Your audience gains social currency in the form of what they experienced. Your brand becomes *the* story: the thing your audience wants to share, and the story others now want to experience for themselves. Your Amazing Brand Story literally walks away with the people who experienced it, for them to spread to new audiences. Now your reputation precedes you.

As a brand marketer, it doesn't get any better than playing a role in creating such experiences. Here's one of my favourites …

Nobody asked us to come to the party

Nike is not a traditional football brand. That's the domain of the German brands, Adidas and Puma – the *authentic* football brands.

In 2005, Nike was a flashy upstart in the football world. Puma had lost its way, and in Australia the gap between the incumbent Adidas and the challenger Nike was significant.

Just like the Nike Running story earlier, the audacious goal within the four walls at Nike's HQ in Australia was to secure the lucrative top spot as the #1 football boot brand as measured by sales.

Some important facts up-front:

- By football I'm talking about soccer as opposed to Aussie rules, league or union.

- At the time, soccer participation numbers in Australia were more than all other football codes combined.

- The target audience was male soccer-obsessed teenagers. We knew if we could position Nike in their eyes as the brand to be seen wearing, the pack would follow.

- However, by boot sales I'm referencing all football boots sold for any football code.

The plan for sales success was anchored in brand success. Nike's product range was incredibly strong, and our sales channels were well established. The focus was on changing the perceptions of the brand in the hearts and minds of those that mattered.

The biggest immediate impact Nike could make was to give a voice to the athletes. Athletes inspire us all to be better versions of ourselves. Athletes are authentic. Through athletes, Nike can attach the brand to emotion – that's its magic.

Hearing the voice of the athlete is what the target audience craved. To be inspired by those who are doing it. To be authentic. To be better.

Therefore, when it came to soccer, the intersection of brand impact and audience desire was Nike Football's brand truth: *Players define where the game is going*.

To make an impact and bring the truth to life in Australia, we knew we had to secure the rights to leverage elite Australian soccer players.

The first thing we did was sign a deal with Football Australia to be the apparel sponsor for the Socceroos. At the same time, we aggressively pursued boot and apparel relationships with all current and potential Australian soccer players, plus the elite Aussie Rules, League and Union players – we knew brand momentum ultimately had to transcend soccer.

Over the next five years, our brand story evolved to reflect the changing fortunes of the Australian players – and indeed, the changing fortunes of Nike football boot sales.

In November 2005, when the Socceroos took to the ground for the FIFA World Cup qualifier in Sydney, Nike was still a distant second to Adidas in sales. But the Nike boot count on the elite players was telling a different story. The 'swoosh' was dominating on pitch. Then we got lucky: the Socceroos qualified for the World Cup for the first time in thirty-two years. The sporting media had a story, and the Nike brand was riding the wave. Images of elite players wearing Nike boots were splashed across the media.

Nobody believed the Socceroos could make an impact at the 2006 FIFA World Cup. Nobody, that is, except the players – their belief was infectious. They spoke about the incredible sense of spirit when pulling on the green and gold – like an armour of relentless ambition to satisfy the burning hunger for respect and recognition. The players believed what they lacked in flair, they made up for with fight. While history would suggest that the Socceroos would be bundled out in the first round, we knew that our players would define where the game is going.

Austin Simms and Sean Jenner, who led our brand communication at the time, knew there was a story to tell. *Stuff History* became our brand story for the 2006 FIFA World Cup. An aggressive campaign brought the story to life as the Socceroos not only made it out of the group stage, but also came within a bootlace of beating the Italians in the quarter finals.

The Socceroos indeed Stuffed History. And the football boot sales figures were beginning to do the same. The gap to Adidas was closing.

With success came expectation. To find the next evolution of the Nike football brand story, we went back to the players.

As a unit, the Socceroos believed that while the flamboyant skills of the European and South American teams are to be admired, they could counter it with grit and determination – the hardened, resilient Aussie spirit. They believed the future was in their hands.

The story Nike told was *Write the Future*. To create lived experiences, we went back to the Nike Football brand truth – *Players define where the game is going*. For the next four years, we were relentless in creating lived experiences that brought this truth to life.

We brought the finest under-18 players in the land closer to the nation's top professional players. We created secret warehouse 3 v 3 tournaments. An under-16 best of the best club competition had the soccer world buzzing. We flew the winners to Manchester United for a week to play at Old Trafford. We teamed elite coaches with elite junior talent in mentor sessions.

During this whole journey the Nike Football story was tracking positively. The big retailers could sense the shifting tide among the influencers. As soon as we saw momentum building, we doubled down.

We created the most rewarding lived experience of all: a talent search for the best unsigned soccer player in Australia. We called it *The Chance*. It was the chance to be discovered and trained by some of the leading coaches in the world. Ron Smith, the former Socceroos technical coach, spotted a gangly seventeen-year-old lad named Tom Rogic. In three short months, Tom went from playing amateur league in Canberra to the global footballing spotlight. Tom's talents and efforts earnt him the ultimate prize of a year at the Nike Football Academy in the UK.

But this was only the beginning of his story. Tom played in the A-League, Australia's most elite club competition. Tom then switched to a European league and became a club star for Celtic in the Scottish Premiership. On debut, he was man of the match. The media called him *The Wizard of Oz*. There were ups and downs, but over time Tom became part of the furniture at Celtic as they strung together seven Scottish Premiership titles in row. All the while, Tom was Nike's poster boy in Australia. He had written his own future – and by no coincidence, we were now within reach of Adidas.

Almost seven years to the day after the Socceroos first wore the Nike strip and qualified for the 2006 FIFA World Cup, Tom Rogic debuted for his country. Again, he lit up the field and became a regular starter and goal scorer for the Socceroos.

Nike's Amazing Brand Story became Tom's Amazing Brand Story, which became the story that every soccer-obsessed teenager was talking about. Experiences create believers.

In 2010, Nike took top spot in football sales from Adidas for the first time ever in Australia. It was a stunning company-wide team effort.

It's easy to lose sight of the seed once the tree has grown. The impact we made was possible because of the brand truth we revealed, the stories we told and experiences we created. Nobody asked us to come to the party. We just arrived with a truth and ruthless determination to win.

Experiences create believers

Great stories are born from great experiences. Designing lived experiences into your offering triggers an emotional response in your audience. In a heartbeat they experience your brand truth. To achieve that, you must give your audience the change they seek.

Like a good night out, the best experiences are often the ones you don't see coming …

I received an SMS from a colleague late one night: *Woody, coffee in Port Melbourne tomorrow morning? Got something we need to see.*

On the way there, Shelley explained to me she'd heard about a creative agency that had opened a café at the base of their building and were using it to experiment with innovative ideas.

It looked like any Melbourne café, full of funky people dressed in dark colours sipping lattes. As the barista passed our morning caffeine fix across the counter, the image of a butterfly chased it.

What the?

When the cup stopped, bright coloured flowers grew out from under my saucer, which attracted more butterflies. I pulled the cup closer. The old flowers wilted and vanished, but new ones sprang up again from under the cup. I was experiencing interactive digital projection for the first time, and I was in awe.

The barista noticed my gaping mouth. *That's a little retail engagement idea we're playing with. It's not quite right yet, but you get the idea.*

In those thirty seconds I knew I had to talk to these people. I wanted to discover what innovation they could help bring to life in Nike stores. The café and agency were See Life Differently, the brainchild of Simon Hammond, a cultural anthropologist and marketing genius.

What I experienced was one example out of hundreds they created every time they opened their doors. In handing over the café to creatives, Simon enabled the story of his agency to play out in the lives of his audience. In Simon's words: *a physical place where hope, ideas, inspiration and new thinking lived.* Now that's a *lived experience* from a business-to-business brand. The story spread like wildfire and filled their sales funnel without ever prospecting or advertising.

Lived experiences flourish when your truth is the compass for innovation and action.

Workbook Exercise 6:

Create lived experiences to make your brand story amazing

Lived experiences are a manifestation of your truth. Therefore, the pathway to creating lived experiences is finding creative ways to bring the truth to life in your business. We use a four-step process to do this:

1. Ask the right question

2. Generate ideas

3. Filter then scope the best ideas

4. Create lived experiences.

Let's look at each step so you're super-clear on the task ahead.

1: Ask the right question

To ensure your ideas are focused, the first thing to do is reframe your brand truth as a positive question. To do this, use your brand truth from Workbook Exercise 3 and replace 'We promise to' with 'How to'. So if your brand truth is: *We promise to deliver first-aid that saves lives*, the question becomes, *How to deliver first-aid that saves lives*. Now your thinking has a sharp focus.

2: Generate ideas

There are two phases to creative thought – *divergent* and *convergent* thinking. Don't let them overlap, as the best ideas will be squashed before they take flight – a little like driving with one foot on the accelerator and the other on the brake.

Start with divergent thinking and let the focused ideas run wild – this is best done in a group workshop environment. Once you have exhausted all ideas, it's then time to apply convergent thinking to cull the bad ideas, then refine and improve the best ones.

There are three provocations to encourage bold thinking in this step:

- If you were starting from scratch, what would you love to do?

- If time and money were no barrier, what would you do?

- What lived experiences would you hate your competitors to create?

3: Filter then scope the best ideas

There's a criteria for filtering the best lived experiences. Amazing lived experiences will do three things:

1. Grow your brand
2. Grow your audience
3. Grow your revenue.

While a lived experience that delivers all three is the holy grail, they are rare, so give priority to ideas that deliver on two of the criteria. Likewise, if there's a knock-out idea that grows your brand (impact) then also consider this.

Some ideas will involve little cost and minimal risk. Others will require investment and may carry greater inherent risks. Complete an evaluation on each of the best ideas to identify all potential risks and mitigation options, as well as the potential rewards that will be generated.

4: Create lived experiences

Now take the simplest of your best ideas and integrate it into your business. It's best to start simple so you and the team quickly build knowledge, confidence, momentum, and belief in using lived experiences. You don't need many lived experiences to make your brand amazing – one or two cracking lived experiences are better than ten average ones.

Remember that being normal and expected do not create experiences that others talk about – being remarkable does.

You're now holding the gold

What you've learnt, and hopefully experienced in this book, has taken me thirty years to understand. Yes, I've had some wonderful successes in creating brand stories, but I've also had my share of failures.

The key thing I've learnt is this: it doesn't matter what you spend on *telling* people about your brand, because if your audience doesn't *believe* it will help them achieve the change *they* seek, you won't win their hearts.

No heart, no story, no connection.

Using lived experiences to connect and stand out takes courage. To design and execute a *lived experience* means saying out loud to the world, *I'm different*. For many, that's awkward.

I find it helpful to remind myself that vulnerability is the portal to creativity, spontaneity, laughter, love, feelings and connection. When we embrace the things that make us different, the rewards can be significant.

The right-hand heist

Belief in yourself and the outcome is paramount to creating growth. I want to share one last story before I leave you.

My grade six teacher was a wonderful educator by the name of Dave Stewart. Mr Stewart had a unique way of bringing mystery to the mundane. His slicked-back silver hair, charismatic charm and off-beat teaching methods paints him in my memory somewhere between a dignified elder and a mad professor.

Mr Stewart didn't teach us about clouds. Instead, he would take the class on a journey of *aliens flying to Earth, passing through some white objects floating in the sky. What were these things? How do they stay up there? What do you mean they are full of water? But where do they come from?*

We would take turns trying to explain to the silver-haired alien what was going on. He would be baffled, throwing chalk in confusion, with the entire class captivated in a fascinating learning adventure.

Dave Stewart knew the power of creating experiences.

Towards the end of grade six, we had a student-teacher join us for a term. Miss McKenzie was the yin to Mr Stewart's yang. Less bluster and show, more intimate and perceptive. We loved her. But something wasn't quite right. When she had to stand up in front of the class, she somehow shrank. This confident woman who had knelt beside us to help work through a task would be like a scared cat, subverting command to the boisterous crowd.

She was no Dave Stewart.

One morning, towards the end of term, Mr Stewart gathered us all together at the start of the day and explained that today was significant. Miss McK was going to be tested. We all looked at Miss McK, who looked like she'd just been told the world was about to end. Mr Stewart explained that another man would be coming into our classroom to observe how Miss McK ran a class and to assess how much we had all learned on the subject she had been charged with teaching us.

Then Mr Stewart stepped down off the raised platform and meandered through our desks like a general readying his troops for battle. He asked us if we all wanted Miss McK to pass the test. We said yes. *Okay*, he said finally, *then here's what we're going to do.*

What happened that day, I'm sure, breaks every rule in the education system. But I suspect it was the experience Miss McK needed, to begin to believe she could be better.

Dave Stewart removed the thing that was holding Miss McK back: the fear of failure. With one simple instruction to the class, he guaranteed that Miss McK could soar.

As close to the word as I can recall, this was Mr Stewart's instruction to us on that day:

Today, and today only, if you know the answer Miss McK asks, you will raise your right hand in silence. If you don't know the answer, you will raise your left hand in silence. Miss McK, you are only to ask answers of those students who raise their right hand. Are we all clear? Can we do this for Miss McK?

Mr Stewart had created a challenge for both the students and student-teacher.

The challenge for us was to beat the system – every child loves to beat the system. We were totally up for it.

Miss McK's challenge was to beat her demons.

The session began. The first question came, and every hand shot up. Half left, half right. The room was silently full of the beaming smirks. Twenty children looking around as the right-hand heist began. *Yes Georgie? Good girl, that's exactly right.*

Soon, correct answers were flying around the room like firecrackers. It felt like we were bank robbers, sneaking the gold out in broad daylight. Right under their noses. With every 'correct' sprouted by Miss McK, she grew in stature. The scared cat began to transform into a lioness right before our eyes. She even stepped off the platform, proudly prowling around her young cubs. She was out-Daveing the great Dave Stewart.

That day we saw a different woman.

According to Mr Stewart, the teaching supervisor's feedback was very positive. Miss McK would indeed have the opportunity to become a great teacher.

Experiences have the power to transform us.

Realness, vulnerability and connection is a linear sequence. If you want to use stories and experiences to stand out, you need to work out what reduces your realness and ability to be vulnerable. Perhaps it's the bravado, the mask, the self-questioning, the little voice that questions why people would listen to you, or perhaps it's the desire to control the outcome. All of these things undermine your ability to be a better storyteller.

The more real, vulnerable and connected you become, the more you multiply the power of your truth. It shifts from intellectual to emotional – from words on a page to stories people tell about you. Vulnerability is your umbilical cord to connection.

Key chapter takeaways

- Stories make people listen. Experiences make people believe.

- Your brand story isn't amazing until it's experienced.

- Your audience will tell stories about their lived experience with your brand.

- Amazing lived experiences will do three things:

  1. Grow your brand

  2. Grow your audience

  3. Grow your revenue.

- Creating lived experiences is the hardest step because it means owning your difference – therefore, a firm belief in the outcome is required.

A parting word

The days of disconnected business and personal worlds are crumbing around us. Organisations and leaders that bring empathy, vulnerability and the power of emotion to the centre of their universe are winning.

Ultimately, we want to feel a connection because as humans we're hard-wired to do so. It's what life is about. We trust the storyteller when they're real – when they know who they are and what their audience wants.

Create Your Amazing Brand Story and go make a difference in the world.

Next steps

The next step for you is simple:

Start.

Work out if you want support and guidance or if you want to do it by yourself – but start.

The energy and clarity of thought you have right now will soon dissipate as you drop back into the fog of life. My advice is to take action now. Your Amazing Brand Story isn't built in one or two sessions – it's crafted and tested over time. Build the momentum. Start at the beginning and create a brand story that will make a positive impact in people's lives and in so doing, make you stand out. The rest will take care of itself.

If you decide you want help, we're here and raring to go:

YourAmazingBrandStory.com

Story log

Stories are a tool to connect with your audience. Influential impact is the end point – stories are just a vehicle to get us there more efficiently and effectively.

Therefore, rather than clog up the contents section of this book with story titles that mean nothing until they're read, I've hidden them here. Essentially this book is a stitching together of twenty different stories, interspersed with metaphors, analogies, exercises, and summaries, to demonstrate and inspire the potential of *Your Amazing Band Story*. Each story serves a purpose. Those stories that were superfluous to the mission (*another twenty*) got the chop.

Here are the stories you read, where they're located, and why they were included:

The story	Chapter	Purpose of the story
The fingerprint	Cover and sleeve	To remind and inspire you of the unique power you hold when you choose to tell your story.
Discovering stories	Introduction	To establish context and connection.
The amazing thing about change	One	To create an elevated perspective, so you can see the potential of your brand story.

The truth about McDonald's	One	To contextualise this elevated perspective in business reality.
The little door of magic	Two	To demonstrate the power of Your Amazing Brand Story to immediately impact your audience.
Soccer, silence and sirens	Two	To provide a case study of a business that applied the formula and doubled their revenue.
Red Nose	Two	To establish the importance of knowing who your target audience is and why.
Connections	Two	To bring all the concepts shared to this point, together and reiterate the key components.
We're not selling doughnuts, people	Two	To demonstrate the commercial power of knowing and leveraging your brand truth.
The rebel	Three	An explanation of how to find and use the right brand emotions.
La vie lente	Three	An example of how Your Amazing Brand Story formula can work in a small business.
A mother's truth	Three	To emphasise the importance of knowing and leveraging your brand's difference.
Character is everything	Three	To bring to life the concept of a brand choosing the frame of reference in which they present themselves.
Good brands walk in the door before you do	Three	To reinforce the benefit of creating Your Amazing Brand Story.

The art and science of storytelling (the heart attack)	Four	To explain the fundamental structure of storytelling and why it works.
The Square Root of Story (The King's Speech)	Four	To provide a visual reference to the classic story arc used to write your brand story.
The Irish inn	Five	To introduce the power of baking lived experiences into your product or service.
Nobody asked us to come to the party	Five	To display the commercial power of brand experiences.
Experiences create believers	Five	To show how a business-to-business brand used experiences to generate word-of-mouth and leads.
The right-hand heist	Five	To inspire you to believe in Your Amazing Brand Story.

Acknowledgements

This book started as a business project, then took a left turn.

What I didn't see coming was the swift transition into a cathartic exploration of what makes me tick. I found it impossible to commit words to a page without questioning why I do what I do, why stories and experiences (and helping others create theirs) are so very close to my heart. Then I realised what was happening … I was searching for my own truth. There's nothing like teaching others to learn about yourself!

I've trusted many people with my stories on this journey. My sincere thanks to those who listened to my yarns and ramblings and the special people to whom I bared my soul. Like rungs on a ladder, you each helped me understand stories and myself a little better. The whole experience has been extremely gratifying.

To the incredibly diverse array of people I've studied and worked alongside over the years who have been a part of the stories I've shared here – you're all awesome. Thanks for making memories with me.

My special thanks to those who read the various early drafts and supported me with such honest feedback. To James Hemmings, Karen Rule, Kirsten Eabry, Shelley Armstrong, Lachlan Wood, HollyAnn Walters-Quan, Rob Richards, Michael Barr, John and Simon Archer, and Theron Vassiliou – I so appreciate you taking the time to care so much and help shape my thinking.

To Sam Trattles and Marcus Pearce for sharing your ups and downs of book writing and self-publishing – your advice has proved very helpful.

To Blaise and Kev at Busybird, thanks for holding my hand through the publishing process. Kev thanks for the amazing fingerprint artwork on the cover. Thanks to Beau Hillier for the beautifully sensitive copy editing and Katrina for spotting my many typos. And to Dave Stokes from author2audio – thanks for your incredible support in recording the audio version of the book.

A big thanks to Lacey and Kevin Fitzgerald for entrusting me to share your family's story and to Red Nose CEO Keren Ludski for the heartfelt confidence.

To Nigel Rideout who was such a font of knowledge and support in my uni days – and who took the time to read an early draft of this book and go back through his journal to recall details (of course you made journal entries) of our 'tea-time' sessions. Thanks, old boy.

To my very old friends Michael Scott and Michal Bloom – our many chats prompted wonderful memories to recall, share and cherish. Bloomy, thanks for laughing so much at my gags still, and Scottie, thanks for your incredible belief and support on the journey.

To Simon Hammond who held my feet to the storytelling fire and helped me straighten out my early drafts, thanks mate.

To Lyndell Pond who has run alongside me in the back half of the writing process and trusted me with her own storytelling journey – thanks a million, my friend.

To Bruce McKaskill, my dear friend and business partner, thank you for challenging me to make this book a story and the countless frank, deep, and incredibly considered conversations that have gently nudged it to where it is. Your generosity in allowing the space to make this happen is so very precious to me.

To our wonderful clients who trust us with their hopes and dreams to grow and make a greater impact – I hope you all see yourselves in the words you helped shape.

To the amazing family I was born into – Mum, Dad, Ray, Brian, Dave and Andy, thank you for your incredible love and support, you all mean the world to me. To my beautiful mother, who is in the advanced stages of wretched Alzheimer's, but who has given me so, so much – thanks for everything Elly, I miss you.

And finally, to my own family with whom I share my love of stories – thanks. To my three amazing children – Harry, Pippa and Jack – who light up my life every day; and the incredibly kind and thoughtful love of my life, Emma, whose unwavering belief helps me more than she'll ever know.

I'm so grateful to you all.

www.ingramcontent.com/pod-product-compliance
Lightning Source LLC
Chambersburg PA
CBHW030332230426
43661CB00032B/1377/J